*Race and Educational Reform
in the American Metropolis*

SUNY Series
FRONTIERS IN EDUCATION
Philip G. Altbach, editor

Race and Educational Reform in the American Metropolis

A Study of School Decentralization

Dan A. Lewis
and
Kathryn Nakagawa

State University of New York Press

Published by
State University of New York Press, Albany

For information, address the State University of New York Press,
State University Plaza, Albany, NY 12246

Production by Bernadine Dawes • Marketing by Dana Yanulavich

Library of Congress Cataloging-in-Publication Data
Lewis, Dan A.
    Race and educational reform in the American metropolis : a study of school
decentralization / Dan A. Lewis, Kathryn Nakagawa.
        p.   cm. — (SUNY series, frontiers in education)
    Includes bibliographical references (p. 181) and index.
    ISBN 0-7914-2133-3 (alk. paper). — ISBN 0-7914-2134-1 (pbk. : alk. paper)
        1. Schools—United States—Decentralization—Case studies.   2. Afro-Americans—
Education—Case studies   3. Education, Urban—United States—Case studies.
I. Nakagawa, Kathryn. II. Title. III. Series.
LB2862.L49   1995
370.19'348'0973—dc20   94-9565
                                                                                 CIP

For Diane and Mick

Contents

List of Tables

Preface

This book is about the education of African Americans in our large cities. We study the largest school systems in the country to see how public school decentralization, aimed at improving the education of minorities, was conceptualized and implemented. The problems of urban education were seen by reformers as matters of power, legitimacy, and participation; as matters of how to design a way of operating school systems that is just and effective. In many cities, the result was decentralization. Our interpretation of this result focuses on the interplay between democracy, bureaucracy, and race, on what Myrdal (1944) called the American Dilemma.

We suggest that the American Dilemma—the reality of segregation in a country that claims adherence to the principles of equality and democracy—fosters decentralization. But decentralization is a result that Myrdal and those who followed in his footsteps (Hochschild 1984; Orfield 1978) never contemplated. Decentralization "solves" the American Dilemma by subordinating African Americans in the competition for educational resources while legitimizing that subordination in terms of equality and power. Whites maintain their hegemony and blacks maintain their "control" of urban institutions like the public school system. The school systems are kept separate and unequal; the racial conflict that sparked integration is transformed

xi

into consensus about the antidemocratic nature of public bureaucracies and the importance of empowering the community (parents included) within the school system.

We reach this conclusion through a political analysis that defines the primary problem of modern politics as the relationship between the centralized bureaucratic state and the decline of democracy (Lipset 1963). Weber (e.g., 1946) and others saw bureaucratic forms of organization eroding democratic institutions and individual freedom. Democratic institutions were no match for the bureaucratic state. What Weber and the earlier theorists could not see was how bureaucratic forms absorbed the democratic critique to support racial and economic relations in the broader society.

We argue that bureaucracy and democracy have merged into a new form of regulation, one that democratizes bureaucracies through functional representation and thereby legitimizes the government (Cawson 1986). The state is transformed and power is dispersed to new interest groups, but within a context that subordinates the cleavage of race to the attack on bureaucracy. Ironically, the result avoids the redistribution of resources and values that was at issue in the original conflict over inequality and segregation in the metropolis. The new decentralized bureaucratic institutions resolve racial conflict and reaffirm racial hierarchy.

The urban school systems of the 1960s exemplified the insulation and nonresponsiveness of bureaucracy run wild. And after attempts at school desegregation had failed, attacks on the bureaucracy began with calls for decentralization. Current discussions of school decentralization[1] are trapped in a conceptual framework that cannot move beyond the shared institutional assumptions of professional educators and reformers. Our theoretical approach crosses several disciplines in an effort to understand educational reform as more than the dreams of progressive individuals. The ideas of reformers matter, but in our framework they end up as tools for those who need to legitimize the subordination. The work of the reformers often supports a new form of regulation, one that rises from the ruins of, and relies on, the old arrangements. It is only in retrospect, when these new arrangements are in place, that we can begin to make out the role reformers played in the transformational period and the nature of the reforms they were promoting.

We relate the school decentralization effort to a general societal movement to "include" marginal groups within the broader institutional protection of civil society and to break the hold of corrupt urban institutions on the life of American democracy. The idea of inclusion also encompasses, in this modern version, the notion of dispersal. Power should be dispersed, given to new interests outside the traditional political system. We use this general framework to analyze changes in the governance of urban public education and to link these changes to race relations. The ideological link between inclusion and urban education is the idea of empowerment.

Reformers have assumed that problems stemmed from the lack of power parents and community members have over the school bureaucracy. Armed with this assumption, they built their reforms on an ideology combining democratic principles of inclusion with institutional critiques of bureaucracy. They sought to deinstitutionalize schooling by empowering the community. By staking reform movements on an ideology of inclusion and deinstitutionalization, school systems were decentralized formally and authority shifted, but without concurrent shifts in resources.

We have organized this book as follows: Chapter 1 lays out the foundation of decentralization through the ideological prism of inclusion and deinstitutionalization. We see decentralization as the reorganization of relations between an urban bureaucracy and the clients it services, one in which the legitimacy of the status quo is affirmed by democratizing the administration of the bureaucracy. In this chapter we question the assumptions underlying this reliance on inclusion and deinstitutionalization. We find that the democratic underpinnings of decentralization are in fact used to support bureaucratic institutions more than to reform them. Finally, we compare empowerment forms of decentralization with less radical enablement forms.

In chapter 2 we contrast our theoretical framework with past analyses of decentralization. In light of the current movements toward decentralization, we find that other explanations are needed to account for patterns of decentralization. Most large urban school systems implemented some form of decentralization over the last twenty years, but the demand for inclusion and decentralization was by no means monolithic. Depending on the political culture of the city and the percentage of the urban population that was black, the demands had very different shapes. The form of decentralization depended in large measure on the political strength of the contending interests in each city and the capacity of those interests to develop an ideology of inclusion that was acceptable to the elites in each political environment.

Chapters 3 and 4 develop in more detail the broad themes from chapter 2. In chapter 3, we begin with a general overview of the movement toward desegregation and decentralization in New York City and Detroit. We then argue that the strength of outsiders and their ability to develop the ideology of inclusion led to empowerment reforms in these cities, but current analyses suggest that decentralization did little to change patterns of either segregation or achievement. In chapter 4 we analyze the decentralization movements in Los Angeles and Dade County and argue that in each case the lack of a coherent outside voice allowed the system to implement a form of decentralization that controlled outside interests from the start.

The creation of these inclusionary systems of urban schooling does not tell the story of how these innovations reproduce the institutional status quo once in operation. Looking at the city of Chicago and its most recent school reform policy, we illustrate in chapters 5 through 8 how decentralization results in support of the status quo. In chapter 5 we utilize interviews with reformers and educational leaders in Chicago to draw a picture of how their strategy of empowerment emerged. We argue that the reformers attacked the school bureaucracy armed with an ideology that specified what parents and community members wanted out of their schools, how they would act once they got into power, and the capacity of those who lost power to pursue their interests. The result was an empowerment model of reform that ultimately allowed the state to vote for change without changing the inequality of resources.

Using data from a survey of Chicago parents, in chapter 6 we suggest that the reformers' assumptions about parents were incorrect—parents in Chicago are much more satisfied with their schools than reformers had depicted. Chapters 7 and 8 detail how the new arrangements introduced by the Chicago school reform left the relations between the races intact because most parents accepted professional control. In interviews with parents who participated in Chicago's most recent school reform, we find that continuity of unequal schooling in Chicago may be explained in terms of the design of the new governance system, the way these new structures worked at the school level, and the types of parents who participated in this empowerment reform.

In chapter 9 we conclude with a discussion of the implications of current forms of decentralization for both race relations and the improvement of urban education.

A word on the support and data collection that drives this study. In 1988 the Spencer Foundation awarded a grant to the first author to study school decentralization in five cities. The data collection for that effort included interviews with elite educational leaders in the five cities, analysis of archival materials, and a random-digit-dialing telephone survey of Chicago parents, as well as in-depth interviews, conducted by the second author, with fifty randomly selected public school parents in Chicago. The results from these interviews and analyses provided the backbone for this book. The data collection, sample, and methodology are described in detail in the Appendix.

NOTE

1. Under the umbrella of "decentralization" we include the terms "community control," "school-based management," and "local school councils."

Acknowledgments

This book was completed with the encouragement and support of a number of organizations and individuals. We thank the Spencer Foundation for its generous support. A Spencer grant provided funding for the study of the different cities and the Chicago parent telephone survey. The School of Education at Stanford University was home for a sabbatical year of reflection and writing for the first author. The friendship and intelligence of Marshall Smith and David Tyack made that year very special. We also wish to acknowledge the continued support of the Center for Urban Affairs and Policy Research at Northwestern University. Needless to say, the conclusions and analysis in this book are the authors' alone and do not represent the positions of the Spencer Foundation or Northwestern University.

Data from the various cities were gathered as part of the School Reform Project at Northwestern University. Members of the research team included Karen McCurdy, Sue Reed, Michael Heise, and Priscilla Wohlstetter. Kristin Carman was an especially important member of the team, providing both research assistance and feedback throughout many stages of the study. Although these individuals were instrumental in conducting this research, responsibility for the final interpretations and conclusions rests entirely with the authors. In addition, we acknowledge Nancy Freedom for her work in compiling the index.

Finally, we wish to thank the educational, community, and political leaders in the cities of our study. They freely gave of their time to participate in our research. We are especially grateful to the Chicago parents who talked about their school reform experience and who took on the challenge of reforming the Chicago public schools.

Chapter 1

Decentralization:
The Ideologies of Inclusion and
Deinstitutionalization

INCLUSION AND THE DEMOCRATIC IDEAL

Isaiah Robinson suggested, almost as a joke, that since white children would not be sent into Harlem schools and black children were not being invited downtown in any meaningful numbers, *maybe the blacks had better accept segregation and run their own schools.* (Fantini, Gittell, and Magat 1970, p. 4; emphasis in original)

African American education historically has been a troublesome issue for white institutions, which often insist on avoiding racial mixing while simultaneously trying to treat people equally. In periods when emphasis on racial equality is strong, some racial mixing is supported, but these brief periods are followed by a return to segregation. Sometimes, as the above quotation illustrates, that segregation is viewed by the segregated group themselves as "unchangeable." Usually, the result is that racial conflict and the demand for inclusion become resolved into a set of arrangements that are legitimate, relatively stable, and anchored in the racial status quo.

Writing in the middle of the twentieth century, Myrdal (1944) described the essential "American Dilemma"—the problem of recon-

1

ciling persistent racial segregation with the American principles of equality and democracy. Myrdal, and later Fredrickson (1971), argued that the African American population has an inferior status in the minds of whites, based on historical relationships of slavery. This deeply ingrained white attitude of black inferiority is the foundation for the desire to keep the races separate. The "inferiority attitude" is not just descriptive but also prescriptive, stimulating whites to build institutions to support their superiority economically and socially. Furthermore, these institutions re-create a sense of "moral hierarchy" in each generation of whites, allowing for the continuation of these racial prejudices.

An early work on urban life and politics illustrates how the inferior status of blacks was maintained and recreated. In *Black Metropolis,* Drake and Cayton (1945) examined segregation in Chicago. They described how blacks migrated to the city, supposedly leaving the system of social control found in the South. Although Drake and Cayton wrote that "Northern institutions...did not have 'keeping the Negro in his place' as one of their primary objectives" (p. 757), they did find a limit on how far blacks could advance in society. Ingrained racial attitudes in the North worked to create a system that, rather than being truly inclusionary, was just as exclusionary, if a bit more subtle, than anything found in the South. Blacks were segregated in the city and kept at the bottom of both the social and the economic hierarchy by a set of institutional arrangements—housing, education, job training—that had a profound influence on their eventual life opportunities.

Ogbu (1978) has extended this line of reasoning in his study of minority education. He has argued that, historically, race relations in the United States are embedded in a caste-like system of economic and social institutions. Blacks were brought to the United States as "involuntary minorities," against their will. Ogbu finds that such caste-like minorities are usually "relegated to menial positions and denied true assimilation into the mainstream society" (Ogbu 1992, p. 8). The caste-like position of blacks has created a lower-quality system of education for them and limits black students to subordinate positions in school and beyond. The involuntary minority status also creates a negative impression of those minorities who choose to achieve—black students who do well in school are often accused of "acting white" and identifying with their white "oppressors." Even then, there is no guarantee of success: "[T]hose who successfully learn to act White or who succeed in school are not fully accepted... nor do [they] receive rewards or opportunity for advancement equal to those open to Whites" (Ogbu 1992, p. 10).

While descriptions of racial subordination such as Ogbu's confirm Myrdal's argument, Myrdal did not think these attitudes were fixed. He felt that the white attitude of superiority would eventually clash with the American belief in democracy. Thus, systems would have to become more inclusionary in order to support the ideology of democracy.

In a democracy, marginal groups must be included in the polity if conflicts are to be settled without resorting to violence and order is to be maintained (Shils 1982). If that incorporation is to lead to stability, there must be a redistribution of power that gives the marginal group a stake in the institutional arrangements (Browning, Marshall, and Tabb 1984). In urban areas, the policy for redistributing power has been inclusion in the form of expanded political participation.

World War II signaled the beginning of the transformation to an inclusionary style of social control. Changes in the domestic economy and the Nazi racial ideology forced the nation to confront the weaknesses of exclusion and segregation (Sitkoff 1978). The federal government and the judiciary were among the institutions targeted in the movement to include black Americans. Civil rights organizations pressured these institutions to bring the practices of the nation in line with its value system. By 1954 the U.S. Supreme Court pushed the inclusionary principle into law with *Brown v. Board of Education,* which outlawed school segregation. During the same period, labor shortages in the North and changes in agricultural practices in the South combined to stimulate the migration of more and more Southern blacks into Northern cities (Lemann 1991).

The increase in the numbers of poor blacks in urban areas eventually led to federal programs aimed at more inclusion. During the mid-1960s, the federal government initiated community action programs (CAPs) as part of the War on Poverty. These programs introduced the concept of "maximum feasible participation," that is, ensuring poor people power in the creation and implementation of the CAPs. However, in many cities inclusion was difficult. Variations in local city politics determined how much inclusion occurred. Greenstone and

Peterson (1968, 1973) found that cities (such as Chicago) that were dominated by entrenched "political machines" were less likely to disperse authority to new agencies. Such cities took black, lower-income political participation less seriously than did other cities, but were able to disperse resources more efficiently. Other, reform-oriented cities allowed more political participation in the running of the CAPs, but were more disorganized and less able to disperse resources and services efficiently. Greenstone and Peterson ironically concluded that "the complete triumph of reform seems to have reduced the political system's capacity to achieve even reformist goals" (1968, p. 290).

In most Northern cities, the public schools were a part of the exclusionary system of social control. Black children went to segregated schools that were often inferior and underfunded when compared to white schools. After *Brown v. Board of Education* in 1954, most large American cities were grappling with the demands of the federal courts and representatives of black interests to desegregate the public schools and equalize the resources spent on those schools. The lack of cooperation from many school districts led community members to other attempts at creating equality of educational opportunity (Scribner and O'Shea 1974). Reformers and community leaders, utilizing the concept of maximum feasible participation, viewed community control and school decentralization as ways to insure that creating equality of educational opportunity was in the hands of blacks, not of the white majority.

Peterson (1985) and Katznelson and Weir (1985) have described how minority groups won inclusion into the public school system by expanding their political power. Peterson has written that Asians and blacks were discriminated against in the education system because they were "politically isolated," that is, they were not part of the "participatory framework." By expanding their power politically, blacks and other minorities believed they could secure better education for their children.

Any kind of political expansion upsets those benefiting from the status quo, and this is particularly true in the educational arena. Historically, reforms in the public education system have never radically altered resource distribution (Katz 1971). The United States has a commitment to "non-socialist approaches to social reform," which eliminates the possibility for policies to equalize income or resources

(Katz 1971, p. 23). Education has thus been used as a prescription for inequalities in society, allowing reformers and others to take part in "a flurry of seemingly purposeful activity" without "tampering with social structures" (Katz 1971, p. 109). We add that the ideology of inclusion as a way of reforming education has also been used to give the *appearance* of change without much resource redistribution. Process replaces outcome as the measure of success.

Within the ideology of inclusion, when marginal groups demand to be part of the institutional center, they are included—but what they thought was the center becomes peripheral to the sources of power. The history of race relations in large American cities can be viewed in this way. African Americans have gained political office in large American cities just as the cities themselves have lost jobs, resources, and authority, not to mention white residents. In a nutshell, this is the story of school decentralization in urban areas. Twenty years ago, decentralization was about being included as a marginal group. Now that blacks and other minorities have gained status in the bureaucratic structures of the public schools, those schools lack resources and status, and the bureaucracy, now largely populated by blacks, is the first to be attacked for educational failure. The center of power in urban public school systems no longer lies in the hands of the bureaucracy; the ideology of inclusion reveals an institutional shell game in American schools, leaving the caretakers bereft of all but the appearance of control.

THE INSTITUTIONAL CRITIQUE

School decentralization, in addition to meshing with general notions of democracy, also met the requirements of the general strategy to reform cities that began in the progressive era. This strategy evolved along traditional reform lines into a way to include peripheral groups while combating institutional corruption and inefficiency. In the early 1960s, these general progressive concerns were tied to the issue of the incorporation of blacks through the struggles for integration and civil rights. That progressive critique, and the emerging coalition that articulated it, pushed for a kind of change that democratized decision making by eroding "machine" control. Inclusion and the resultant powers for decision making were dispersed to newly formed interest groups that argued for a type of reform that focused on *procedures for* making decisions rather than the *substance of* those decisions. In cities where politics were dominated by issues of race, the business elites, legislators, and media were won over to this way of thinking. The revised ideology of reform, supported by conservative business interests, evolved into a set of organizations that purported to speak for the educational needs of the black poor. And the insiders—that is, the bureaucratic leadership of the schools—failed to adjust their thinking to the critique. The natural result was that "insiders," or school bureaucrats, came into conflict with "outsiders," or reformers and other progressive groups (Crain 1969).

Government service bureaucracies, historically, have controlled the amount of inclusion and political participation in their institutions. But in the 1960s, newer forms of citizen involvement emerged to respond to problems of inclusion. Banfield and Wilson (1963) found that many urban reformers during the early sixties called for arrangements that shifted power away from political machines and electoral parties and toward new nonpartisan forms of organization. Urban reformers sought a transition to more middle-class forms of governance away from the corrupt political machines of the first half of the century. In response to racism, corruption, and inefficiency, urban reform passed from a reliance on electoral innovations (e.g., nonpartisan elections or referenda) to an investment in democratic participatory mechanisms. The demand for racial equality was transformed into the demand to reorganize bureaucratic decision making. The American Dilemma became bureaucratized.

Banfield and Wilson (1963) believed that government served two purposes: to deliver services and manage conflicts. They acknowledged that services were sometimes the mechanism for managing conflicts, but they did not foresee that conflicts could be submerged in the delivery of services. By reorganizing how services, such as schooling, are delivered, the government effectively alleviates conflicts by suppressing them.

Conflict among groups keeps a democracy working, provided that conflict can be kept within acceptable bounds. The level of acceptability is controlled by elites who determine the extent to which, and the means by which, an aggrieved group is absorbed into the institutional structure of the society. The question is not just when the new groups gain access to political power (Lipset 1963), but how. By the end of the 1960s that new access and inclusion was being defined through the prism of a white urban reform agenda that focused on what we call "democratic proceduralism" (Lewis, Grant, and Rosenbaum 1988). These white reformers were attempting to break the hold of political machines on large cities by creating new processes through which African Americans could exert some control over urban political and service institutions. Blacks had to be included, but included by changing the procedures used to make decisions in the service bureaucracies.

The relationship between democracy and bureaucracy is fundamental to much of the discourse about advanced capitalist societies, but most of that debate has been about how bureaucracies and the elites they breed undermine democratic institutions (Burnham 1943). We are interested in the inverse relationship, that is, how democratic tendencies are used to support bureaucratic institutions and the socioeconomic relations they protect. The literature (Piven and Cloward 1971; Selznick 1949) has focused on cooptation and participation, and the undermining of representative government in its more traditional forms.

What we find are two parallel critiques imperfectly blended into school decentralization. On the one hand, there is the ever-present racial conflict and the resultant demand for democracy and inclusion. On the other hand, there is the bureaucratic institutional critique, which attempts to transform some bureaucracies even as they become more inclusionary. School decentralization was a *reorganization* of relations between an urban bureaucracy and its clients, where the legitimacy of the schools was affirmed by democratizing the administration of the bureaucracy. Such reorganization supported minority demands for power without redistributing educational benefits between whites and blacks. The institutional critique, coupled with inclusion, legitimized the unequal distribution of resources and the continued separation of the races in the name of transforming the bureaucracy.

American reliance on an institutional analysis is rooted in a political philosophy that emphasizes rationalism, a benign human nature, and the notion that evil behavior flows from poorly designed institutions (Burnham 1985). Rational solutions to difficult problems could be found in the rearrangement of the organizations that claim expertise over the problem. This view promoted the idea that men and women could be changed by these organizations, and social problems solved. In the late 1950s and 1960s, foundations and federal programs turned these beliefs into policy as they aimed to improve how human services operated by forcing them to turn outward to meet the challenges of poverty and race relations. Up until that time, bureaucracies, especially school systems, were not responsive to the needs of the poor (Marris and Rein 1967). In creating new policies to help the poor, reformers assumed that rational reform could achieve its ends, that human nature was at worst malleable and would respond to institutional shifts in activity, and that better-designed institutions would work better. In terms of public education, changing how the schools operated would change the educational chances of the poor.

However, as public bureaucracies resisted reform efforts, institutional analysis led to calls for deinstitutionalization. Theories of deinstitutionalization have their foundation in the Chicago school of sociology. Goffman (1961) and Becker (1963) adapted earlier theories on occupational careers to the worlds of deviance and institutions. Their theories were built on issues of identity formation and interpersonal interaction as formulated by the founders of American sociology. Personal identity was based on how others related to you. You were who others said you were. If institutions were total, then who you were followed from the roles you played institutionally. Systematic changes in occupational identity were the result of role expectations and institutional needs. The institution created a career. Goffman and Becker applied this approach to the bottom rather than the top of the organization. Where others had looked at how medical careers were formed in the 1940s, these scholars looked at the patient career in the 1950s. Deviance was not in the personality of the criminal or mental patient; rather, it was in the institutional definitions applied to those it recruited to the patient role.

If institutions by definition created the very people they were supposed to change, then reform meant destroying the factories of deviant identity and failure. This theory was supported by empirical work in the institutions of social control that were overflowing in the 1950s. Large, crowded, and understaffed, these places came to be seen as the cause of problems. They had to be radically transformed.

Schools are not quite "total institutions" (Tyack 1974); they do not have complete control over the lives of students. Students go home at the end of the day, they skip school, they transfer out, and they have alternative sources of identity provided by peers, parents, and others. But the public schools do have many features in common with other institutions, and the deinstitutionalization paradigm was a powerful ideological tool for understanding social problems. In the late 1970s, Meyer (1977) adapted institutional analysis to the formal study of schooling, arguing that myths and institutionalized rules drive schooling and its organization far more than do science and performance.

Thus, as the movement to reform urban schools in the late 1960s gained moral advantage from the ideals of democracy and inclusion, the movement also gained political support from an ideology of deinstitutionalization. Fantini, Gittell, and others used this perspective to shape a reform strategy for public schooling which insisted that the bureaucracy was the problem, and that external control by the "community" was the solution, thus combining the two perspectives of inclusion and deinstitutionalization. For Fantini, Gittell, and Magat (1970) "the institution" meant the set of arrangements—bureaucratic, professional, and centralized—by which public education was delivered. Public schooling had been taken out of politics by these institutional forces, and the city reformers of the late 1960s wanted to put politics back in (Rogers 1968). If the institution was controlled politically by outside forces, schooling would improve.

The reform dilemma was articulated as a choice between two institutional systems: one operated by the community and open, and one operated by professionals and closed. Open up the institution and you fix the problem. An institution could generate either learning or failure, depending on how it was designed; in broad terms, change who runs the bureaucracy, and the life chances of the clients would improve.

FROM DEINSTITUTIONALIZATION TO EMPOWERMENT

Like reformers of other human services, big-city school reformers believed in the deinstitutionalization ideology. The school bureaucracy, like other bureaucracies, was failing to respond adequately to the demands for change that were made by local and national elites (Peterson 1976; Rogers 1968). As more modest projects to improve the schools failed to achieve the objectives that were set for them, and desegregation efforts met massive resistance in large American cities, commitment to the notion that the bureaucracies could improve themselves without outside control lost legitimacy. Professionals and the bureaucracies that housed them were seen as incapable of improving the situation. Like mental hospitals and prisons, schools were transformed in the name of community.

The idea of maximum feasible participation carried with it a commitment to empowerment. Schools, the welfare department, and other agencies were supposed to improve the relative position of their clients, and there was ample evidence that they were failing to do this. Indeed, some argued that these services contributed to keeping the poor at the bottom of the socioeconomic ladder by making them more dependent on the very services that were supposed to help them and thus less capable to compete (Ogbu 1978). The core of the dilemma came to be seen as the lack of power that the poor had over these agencies of improvement. Increasing the participation of the poor in the governance of these services would lead to empowerment.

The War on Poverty in the 1960s created a national policy built on these assumptions. During this period, social services were aimed particularly at helping children in poverty, and programs such as Head Start helped children by helping the children's families (Zigler and Valentine 1979). Although this was similar to the mainstreaming of immigrant groups during the 1920s, in this case the groups to be mainstreamed were the poor and rural minorities who had migrated to urban centers (Gordon 1977; Slaughter and Kuehne 1988). The empowerment focus meant that in programs like Head Start, where parents played an integral role, parent education and training were supplemented with parent involvement in the running of the program (Valentine and Stark 1979). The participatory democracy ideal was utilized in Head Start to empower parents so they would learn to have control over factors that affected them, and in that way they could improve themselves and the lives of their children.

As with Head Start, parent empowerment in the schools was anchored by the idea that empowerment would change both the lives of the participants and the running of the institution:

Both the schools and the parent and community participants themselves benefit from their active involvement in the education process.
Their very act of meaningful participation—a sense of greater control
over a decisive institution that influences the fate of their children—
contributes to parents' sense of potency and self-worth. (Fantini, Gittell, and Magat 1970, p. 95)

The reformers of the 1960s believed that improved self-worth of the
parents would also improve the lives of the children. And the end
product of these improvements would ultimately be educational
achievement (Gittell and Hevesi 1969; Levin 1970).

A study by HARYOU (Harlem Youth Opportunities Unlimited,
Inc.) in 1964 offered some of the first ideas for empowerment and
community control. Titled "Youth in the Ghetto: A Study of the Consequences of Powerlessness and a Blueprint for Change," the research
detailed both quantitatively and qualitatively the status of Harlem
youth. Clark (1965) used the findings to raise questions about social
power and how the schools might be changed to allow the "youth in
the ghetto" both educational and social power. As Gittell and Hevesi
(1969) wrote in applying this notion to the schools:

The accumulated evidence indicates a basic sickness in the school
structure: The total environment of the system prevents progress and
changes that would meet new situations and serve new populations.
Studies...have identified as the fundamental malady an insensitive system unwilling to respond to the demands of the community. (p. 8)

If the poor had control of the schooling enterprise, these scholars
argued, then they could make it work by directing the educational
effort toward the goals of those being served. Carmichael and Hamilton (1967), in their book *Black Power: The Politics of Liberation in
America,* strongly stated the case: "Black parents should seek as their
goal the actual control of the public schools in their community: hiring and firing of teachers, selection of teaching materials..." (p. 166).
Professionals would respond to the authority of the new governance
structure or they would be removed. If the community (meaning people who live near the school) and parents of school-age children had
more voice in the schooling enterprise, there would be more parent

satisfaction with the schools and more commitment to the educational process. The result would be improved educational attainment. The democratization of the governance process and the representation of parent and community interests would be both a cause and a consequence of "empowerment."

Not only would individuals become empowered, but it was assumed the school bureaucracies that controlled access to opportunities would be more responsive when parents and community members governed their own schools (Mayor's Advisory Panel on Decentralization 1969; Carmichael and Hamilton 1967; Glass and Sanders 1978; LaNoue and Smith 1971; Levin 1970). The approach hinged on several unspoken assumptions about social and political change that were sorely tested in the ensuing decade as these efforts met stiff opposition and failed to meet many of their goals.

The first assumption was that if the school bureaucracy performed better, then individual mobility would follow. The assumption proved untenable as issues of race and class in labor markets and residential segregation proved far more intransigent than originally thought (Marris and Rein 1967). The second assumption was that school governance was related to student achievement. Not only was this difficult to measure, but, with respect to parent empowerment, Fine (1993) asserts there is no link between increased parent power and increased student achievement. The third assumption was that power and authority could easily be transferred by legislative action; such an assumption vastly underestimates entrenched modes of bureaucracy and the distribution of resources (Gruber and Trickett 1987). The final assumption was how the individual parents would respond to such a policy—that they wanted decision-making responsibility and that it would lead to more parental commitment to the institution (e.g., volunteering, helping with homework, even building up parents' own skills and educational interests). Research (Wasley 1993) does not indicate that parents necessarily want decision-making responsibility; however, increased involvement in the school has been related to increased commitment (Fine and Cook 1992).

In deinstitutionalization, parents are treated as agents of change with common interests in how the schools should be operating. In essence, the empowerment model, which rests so heavily on the importance of outside interest groups, treats parents themselves as an interest group. These parents can articulate shared interests in opposition to the interests of other groups or classes that also seek to control the educational process, especially if they are aided by reformers and activists who can help articulate those interests. If the governance structure changes to accommodate those parental interests and treats the parents with respect, then parents will soon be able to articulate their own interests and develop their own leadership. Community organizations that represent those parent interests are important in the reform process, for they teach parents not to accept the powerlessness that professionals impute to them, and they draw parents together to act politically. The empowerment model suggests that parent dissatisfaction with urban education and parent involvement in the school are related, and that under the right circumstances parents with strong community ties and the right values will get involved with schools (Bastian, et al. 1986; LaNoue and Smith 1973).

EMPOWERMENT VERSUS ENABLEMENT

The empowerment model is not the only approach to urban school reform. In contrast to the empowerment model, which sets out the school as the problem, the enablement approach shifts the onus of change onto the family. In its current guise the enablement model is based on an analysis of how societal forces are changing the family and how the schools must do a better job of relating to those families. While there is much talk of sensitivity and partnership, the impetus for change comes from teachers and bureaucrats, the very interests the empowerment paradigm sees as the cause of the problem.

In the enablement approach, school professionals are urged to change themselves so they can better accomplish the ends of schooling, and these same professionals are given resources to reach out to the community and draw it into the schooling enterprise. Power is not the problem—some might need more of it and others have abused it—but rather social change (i.e., increased poverty, advanced technology) has made the schools' job harder. This approach is often critical of the school bureaucracy but suggests that the bureaucracy can fix itself and be more responsive to parents. In the enablement model, governance is less an issue than is the creation of incentives to get the bureaucracy to mend its ways by reaching out to and including parents in the educational endeavor. Enablement advocates seek to get parents involved in, and committed to, what the school is trying to do—educate the child for a productive role in the society. Coleman (1990) describes how schools should operate in an enablement approach:

> [P]arents are unskilled in helping their children to succeed in school. Even well educated parents often lack the knowledge of what practices in the home will be most helpful to their children in succeeding in school.... It thus becomes in the school's own interest to strengthen these social resources. (p. 25)

Whereas the empowerment camp emphasizes *power* over the educational enterprise, the enablement approach pushes for more parental *commitment* to the educational enterprise. In the latter model, the school reaches out to parents to overcome the alienation of the educational process. The enablement approach, to its credit, recognizes that commitment will come only if schools make parents welcome at the school. In that model, parents should be taught how to help their children learn better and support what the school is doing educationally (Comer 1986; Epstein 1985). Educational professionals can make this happen through enlightened programming and innovative leadership.

Coleman (1990), Comer (1980), and Lightfoot (1978), although coming from different directions, exemplify the enablement approach. Each implicitly assumes that the people who run the bureaucracies have an interest in improving their operation and will be moved to action by the desire to achieve the formal goals of public education. They also assume that even though national societal and economic trends might be responsible for the problem of poor school achievement, activities at the local school can reverse these societal trends. Studies of reforms at schools and other socialization and resocialization agencies make it clear that other priorities (e.g., load shedding) influence how managers and street-level bureaucrats go about their jobs but that a recommitment to educational values is possible. Case studies in educational reform suggest that leadership can make a difference (Purkey and Smith 1983).

This approach to parent participation focuses on school personnel's developing ways to involve parents in the education of their children that supplement the activities of the teacher and the school (e.g., Becker and Epstein 1982; Coleman 1990; Comer 1980). Rather than being for political ends, participation is for educational ends. As with the empowerment model, structural problems in the system are treated as relationship problems. Teachers and principals work with parents to draw them into the educational activities of the school, sometimes by giving parents a voice in those activities. Here the teacher is looking for ways to put the parent to work as a resource for the education of the child, getting him or her committed to the values of education and working out a more collaborative arrangement between the school, the parents, and the community.

School-based management (SBM) is the decentralization policy that exemplifies an enablement model. In a district that has adopted SBM, local administrators and teachers have more power over their individual schools (allowing the bureaucracy to fix itself) (Cistone, Fernandez, and Tornillo 1989). Usually parents have an advisory role in such policies, and they are often viewed as a "program"—as in creating parent education classes or in having parent networks (Brown 1990; Caldwell and Spinks 1988; Lighthall 1989).

We exaggerate the differences between enablement and empowerment policies in order to differentiate their underlying assumptions. Enablement policies such as school-based management often use the term *empowerment* with respect to teachers and staff rather than parents and community (Rungeling and Glover 1991). And empowerment advocates state that community control would empower not only parents but also school staff (Bastian et al. 1986).

Fundamentally, enablement and empowerment views differ in their beliefs as to whether the system can reform itself or needs outsiders to do it. When Bastian and colleagues (1986) discuss "democratic schooling" as their aim, they do not believe in the system. They cite as the main deficiencies of the public educational system a "crisis of inequality" and a "crisis of citizenship," and they state that "progressive reform therefore requires empowering the constituents of schooling as both essential elements of school culture and indispensable agents for change" (p. 165). Bastian includes teachers as part of the community, but she and her colleagues are pushing for parents and community to become necessary parts of the process—in fact, they cite the work done by Designs for Change (the community organization that spearheaded the Chicago school reform) as an example of their philosophy.

In contrast, Comer's plan, detailed in his book *School Power* (1980), emphasizes parent inclusion in the schooling process, but still leaves professionals in charge. Comer's philosophy is that "parents are more likely to support a school program in which they are partners in decision-making and welcome at times other than when their children are in trouble" (p. 70). Comer addresses educational practices of the staff more than prerogatives of the parents. And in fact, although Comer believes a school is better when parents are involved, he has also admitted that parent involvement is not always necessary for school improvement:

> I acknowledge that schools can be improved without significant parent participation. Indeed, because of cutbacks in Chapter 1 funds, we have sharply reduced parent participation in our two earlier project schools, and the high level of achievement has continued. (1986, p. 446)

Both the enablement and the empowerment models have driven reform in several large cities over the last twenty years. The power of each depends in large measure on the relative strength of interest groups in differing locations. The competition between insiders and outsiders for control over the reform agenda determines the hegemonic ideology. In the next chapters, we will describe how decentralization emerged in the empowerment cities and suggest how the politics of each city interacted with the ideological dimensions we have discussed to produce a decentralized system of school governance. We will then describe the decentralization that took place in the enablement cities and show the factors that account for that approach to reform.

Ironically, with its concentration on allowing professionals to change themselves, the enablement approach might result in a better distribution of resources. Dade County, where we find the strongest example of an enablement policy, seems more capable of raising educational outcomes than are any of the empowerment cities. Like the machine politics cities of the 1960s, the professionals in Dade County are better able to understand the system and distribute resources to school sites than are the parents and community in empowerment cities.

DECENTRALIZATION IN THE 1990s

During the 1980s, the dispersal of power legitimized the separation of whites and blacks. But more recently decentralization has divided the black middle class from the black poor. In the current educational arena the conflict between middle-class and lower-class minorities is exacerbated. The inclusionary ideal of the 1960s opened the system up to many black professionals, drawing them inside the bureaucracy. The outsiders pushing for more reform today are business groups and reform organizations. They call for grassroots decision making, bypassing the black middle-class school professionals. They accept budgetary limits. In cities with large minority populations, the result is a handicapped system of governance, where black school professionals have little capacity to harness and articulate the interests of the poor, let alone improve the capacity of the schools to do their job. The dispersal of power makes a clear statement of goals and the exercise of leadership difficult. This leads to an empowered urban school system that is hamstrung vis-à-vis state officials.

In a sense, these splits along class lines further highlight the tension between enablement and empowerment. Enablement reformers have faith in black professionals as educators, whereas empowerment advocates still seek to discredit the bureaucracy regardless of who the professionals are. The inclusion of the past is undermined as the power of minority parents is pitted against minority professionals, eroding a strong coalition along racial lines. In the 1960s, Charles Hamilton posed the fight over decentralization as a question of legitimacy or efficacy. He argued that black parents were calling for community control because the school system was not a legitimate public institution. At that time, public education was controlled by whites: few blacks were professionals in the system, and the institution did not represent black interests. Whites, on the other hand, believed in the viability of the system, but questioned its efficacy and so sought reforms (such as changes in the curriculum or new school programs) that made the existing system more effective.

Today, urban education is a minority enterprise. Whites have withdrawn and taxpayers in general are loath to spend. Decentralization is the ideology that legitimizes the current situation. In the pages to come we will describe how this situation developed and what factors account for the variations we find between enablement and empowerment cities. Divisions between blacks and whites have been eclipsed by divisions between centralizers and decentralizers. The result is an educational system that supports the racial hierarchy.

Chapter 2

Big Cities and Patterns of Decentralization

School decentralization has taken center stage in our largest cities as central administration and bureaucracy are increasingly viewed as the source of educational problems. New York City and Detroit two decades ago, and Los Angeles, Chicago, and Miami/Dade County in the last few years, are all involved in major school reforms that pivot on breaking the hold of central bureaucracy on decision making. The newer generation of reforms appears even more participatory and grassroots-oriented than the older ones, with individual schools having the authority to hire principals and set educational policy.

Existing theories of urban politics and school reform provide a start in deciphering this phenomenon. Researchers such as Piven and Cloward (1971) and Katznelson (1981) have emphasized the regulatory role of government in controlling the aspirations and demands of the poor. Their central focus was on how outside organizations articulated the demands of the poor and pursued their interests. Although these scholars applaud the efforts of reform groups in winning the reforms, this approach has not been used to understand how the process worked that resulted in school decentralization.

"Social control" theorists in urban education focus on the functions that public education plays in the maintenance of the economic system, reproducing both legitimacy for the system and a compliant

19

labor force (e.g., Bowles and Gintis 1976). This approach has been used to analyze a variety of urban policies (e.g., Greenstone and Peterson 1973) and has been useful in historical studies of urban schooling (Katznelson and Weir 1985), but it has not been applied by political scientists to current issues of urban school reform. These important historical studies describe the way reforms supported and legitimized changes in schooling policy, while appearing to improve the position of poor and working people.

Social control theorists have been less willing to turn their critical analysis to contemporary reforms. Bastian and colleagues (1986) are an exception to this rule, but they write as advocates of democratic reforms for the lower class, while criticizing other reforms, such as the "excellence" movement, which they see as supporting business interests. Indeed, many radical educational scholars have found themselves arguing for decentralization efforts as remedies for the bureaucratic stagnation and the insulation of schools from popular control. Gittell and Rogers and their colleagues were eloquent critics of the New York City school system bureaucracy, and the most adept chroniclers of the transition to the decentralized system. In Detroit, Dimond (1985) looked at the desegregation battle and Glass and Sanders (1978) described the transition to the decentralized system in the early 1970s, but these researchers did so from more conventional pluralist perspectives. The social control thinkers who have written in Detroit have not focused on schooling per se and have looked more at the overall economic development of the city and the region.

Peterson (1976) has put considerable skill and effort into understanding school politics. His important book on Chicago finds that controlled combat between ethnic and racial groups produces policy outcomes for the city, with the school board defined as the arena in which these conflicts are resolved. Conventional notions of power, based on resource control, shape who wins and loses in these conflicts. Yet the actors Peterson focused on, such as the school board and the union, were all but irrelevant to the current Chicago reform debate and outcome, as state legislators and outside reformers called many of the shots.

The work of Easton (1965), modified and applied by Scribner and O'Shea (1974), depicted school politics in terms of demands on a system and the system's response to the demands. Among educational researchers there has been a focus on the administrative and political difficulties that school officials face in cities (e.g., Ornstein 1973). Approaches such as these assume an educational policy arena in which the combat between powerful groups, from both inside and outside the system, determines educational outcomes.

LaNoue and Smith (1973) provided a comprehensive study of the politics of decentralization, describing many of the factors that lead to the process of decentralization. They, like other researchers (Boyd and O'Shea 1975; Scribner and O'Shea 1974), saw changing demographics, failed attempts at integration, low school achievement, and strong outside coalitions as preexisting conditions that would lead to decentralization. Boyd and O'Shea (1975) emphasized that decentralization would not be considered as a policy if a "crisis of authority" did not already exist in the system. When a system is in such a state of crisis, it might either respond to outside pressures or do some internal "boundary spanning" to head off outside demands for change. If a school system takes action, administrative (enablement) decentralization is implemented; if the system waits to react, community control (empowerment) is often the result.

To some extent, such analyses of decentralization still hold up today. Our study of Chicago found a great deal of dissatisfaction with the system and a strong outside representation of interests, and the result has been an empowerment policy of decentralization. However, there are three key differences between these earlier analyses and the politics of decentralization today. First, unlike the cases of Detroit and New York, school officials have played a more marginal role in the reforms. Second, communities are no longer reacting to failed attempts at integration—most urban systems are so dominated by minorities that integration is no longer on the policy agenda. Third, the school bureaucracy is no longer dominated by whites; in many urban systems the board and superintendent, as well as many administrators and teachers, are minority.

RECONCEPTUALIZING SCHOOL DECENTRALIZATION

As we outlined in chapter 1, the key to our perspective on urban school reform is the recognition that decentralization signals a change in how society regulates marginal groups. The United States has moved from an exclusionary approach of social control to one that regulates through "inclusion" into society. Much like the transformation of social control institutions to a segregative system in the early nineteenth century, the current transition is to a new set of institutions that includes deviants and marginal groups. This transition began in the mid-1950s and has affected many of our regulatory systems over the last thirty years. Inclusionary approaches are often promoted as important innovations in how we care for and help people, but we are more interested in how they actually function and who gains and loses as these new systems of social control expand.

This transition to inclusion is often described as a "community" alternative to the rigid bureaucratic way of doing business. *Community mental health, community corrections,* and *community crime prevention* are the names given to the inclusionary push in other sectors of the social control apparatus. Regardless of the name, it is part of a society-wide effort to move regulation toward services and procedures that control deviant groups by integrating them into civil society. Let us hasten to add that this inclusion brings with it a new legitimacy for the social control apparatus, while at the same time creating new mechanisms for maintaining stratification and hierarchy within the society.

Many of the scholars who study these issues are advocates for the reforms that are being introduced, and thus use the very categories they should be scrutinizing as concepts for assessing the new systems of regulation. The result is studies that support the ideology of inclusion and move the transformational process along. There are, of course, important variations in how this inclusion is accomplished in different social control sectors. Prisons, mental hospitals, and juvenile correctional facilities have all been changed by this process. Much of the research in these areas is supported by the federal government and centers on how to make the reforms work.

Contemporary school reforms are part of this inclusionary revolution that is changing the face of American society and the ways we regulate marginal groups. In their exclusionary phase, large city school systems treated outside pressure to improve the schools as illegitimate, especially when it came from those who represented blacks whose children were being segregated and who were critical of the quality of the schooling they were experiencing. Early studies of large city school systems found that the insulated nature of power allowed school systems to sidestep, rather than respond seriously to, such pressures. It was not until central institutions outside the school system—such as courts, legislatures, and the media—pressed for increased minority representation, that school systems began to include blacks and other minorities in governance decisions about the schools and to reduce the independence of school bureaucracies. Reform organizations, with foundation and federal support, began to emerge in the early seventies to articulate the demand for minority inclusion.

In retrospect, the political struggles over desegregation and community action programs (and now decentralization) all seem to have been less about political empowerment and more about the transition to a new "hierarchical biracialism" (Fredrickson 1971) form of inclusion. Fredrickson suggests that the debate on the place of African Americans in early twentieth century American society is framed by a belief that blacks and whites should be kept separated in order for the latter group to maintain its competitive advantage over the former. Today's decentralized school systems continue to promote this hierarchy, keeping the races separated while turning demands for political equality into a matter of bureaucratic participation. Black interests are represented in ways that support the service economy. If blacks are to be kept apart in the name of subordination, if they are now more useful as "clients" than as cheap labor, then institutional arrangements had to allow for their subordination outside labor markets in the North. This must also be done within the value system of the polity, supporting equal rights and democratic institutions, but not allowing for too much redistribution. Not only are incorporation and racial separation compatible with decentralization, the latter makes the former possible. In cities where blacks and other minorities are less threatening to white interests because their numbers are smaller and their political power weaker, incorporation follows an enablement model, building the power of unions and superintendents while attacking centralization and bureaucracy.

In cities where minorities have become a majority, the demand for political inclusion is met with a kind of decentralization that disperses political power and makes it very unlikely that institutional power will develop. And where it does develop, the chances of getting support from elites outside the city is slim—as has been seen in Detroit. In other cities, like New York and Chicago, empowerment movements develop because white power structures must somehow accommodate black demands for more inclusion and power over the institutions that shape their lives. But often empowerment emerges in ways that leave suburban areas unaffected and represents interests in ways that disengage the call for legitimacy from the demand for redistribution. This decoupling follows from the *dispersal* of power through decentralization.

The dispersal of authority beginning in the 1960s was set against the background of racial change and the political culture of each city. The history of that change and the political context of the cities can be separated into two types of urban experience: empowerment cities and enablement cities. The empowerment cities are located in the Midwest and Northeast and share similar racial histories while varying significantly on how their political cultures handled the issue of inclusion. The enablement cities share similar racial histories and a progressive political culture that emphasizes nonpartisan reform procedures. In the empowerment cities we focus on—New York City, Detroit, and Chicago—the dispersal that began in the 1960s was characterized by a challenge to the power of professionals and the bureaucracies that focused on political definitions of the problem and a conflict mentality toward the resolution of the issues. The dispersal of power took a political direction, focusing on governance issues and giving power to something called the "community" in contrast to the school bureaucracy.

In the enablement cities (Los Angeles and Miami/Dade County), the focus was on how the schools could be reorganized to assimilate the parents and the community. Here power remained in the bureaucracy and the issues were framed in terms of administrative changes that could improve operations. Teachers and a sympathetic superintendent led to a coalition that provided decentralization as the procedure for improving schooling. The political culture of progressivism and the political weakness of black organizations led to changes that increased the power of professionals while dispersing the power of other groups.

Both types of decentralization—enablement and empowerment—have been analyzed before (e.g., Cohen 1973; Ornstein 1973, 1983), but few studies have explored the variations between cities in the type of decentralization in operation. Crain (1969), in his work on school desegregation, was one of the first to examine the determinants of school reform decisions. His study of school board decision making led to the notion that a city's political style, that is, the relationship between the civic elite, elected officials, the citizenry, and special interest groups, predicted the eventual school board stance toward desegregation. Crain's notion of a city's political style is useful in studying the link between the educational power structure and decentralization reforms (Wohlstetter and McCurdy 1991). In particular, we draw on Crain's work to identify particular factors across the cities that differentiate their processes of reform. We are drawn to the views of school elites in each city to ascertain how key groups define issues and work together.

LOOKING AT THE CITIES

As a context for our study of Chicago, and to look at the patterns of decentralization and the relations between the actors, we conducted interviews between the fall of 1988 and the spring of 1989 as part of the School Reform Project. The project studied reform in five school systems: Chicago, Miami/Dade County, Detroit, Los Angeles, and New York City. Visits were made to each city, and 117 educational-elite interviews were conducted. The interviews were semistructured, consisting of a mixture of questions focused on educational reform. See the Appendix for more information on methodology and sample.

We chose these cities for two main reasons. Their problems may be equated with what most of us call "urban education," and each has grappled with how to reform itself to be more responsive to minority concerns. A large percentage of African Americans or other minorities live in these cities, and their experiences shape what goes on in other urban areas. We have also selected these cities because decentralization has emerged in them as an important innovation around which there has been considerable debate and action. In two of the cities, New York and Detroit, decentralization has been in effect for more than two decades and has become the policy environment in which debates about schooling take place. In three other urban systems, Dade County, Los Angeles, and Chicago, decentralization has been introduced in the last few years as an innovation that can change and improve schooling.

These are also five cities in which the drama of race relations has been played out over the last thirty years. From riots in the sixties to mayoral elections in the eighties, to riots again in the nineties, blacks and whites have struggled with the dilemma of how to live together in these cities. We are interested in the variations of racial politics that we find in these cities, for they set the parameters and conditions for what is possible. Race and authority in educational politics have played out their possibilities in these cities with important consequences for the definition of urban school reform.

Much of the debate over urban policy and especially race relations has also developed in these areas, and many of the experiments that have guided both school policy in particular and urban policy in general were started in these systems. Scholars have also spent a great deal of time comparing these urban sites, their politics and their policy outcomes (although Dade County is a less developed site for social science research). Indeed, relying on the work of others, we see how incorporation and dispersal became the twin features of urban policy and shaped the movement toward decentralization.

In analyzing our data, we differentiated between "insiders," or actors within the system—the board, general superintendent, and teachers union—and "outsiders," such as reform organizations and city and state political leaders. We found (as have others, e.g., Boyd and O'Shea 1975) that where outsiders were extremely critical of the system, a form of empowerment decentralization had been enacted, whereas when outsiders lacked a uniform critical voice, a form of enablement decentralization had been implemented. This confirmed Crain's finding in that the type of decentralization enacted was dependent upon the political style—the relationships among the educational elite—of a city.

In all three of the empowerment cities we studied (New York City, Detroit, and Chicago), civil rights groups had organized to demand the desegregation of the schools. Organizations banded together as coalitions, drawn by an interest in desegregation but little else. By 1963 both New York and Detroit had brought in liberal white superintendents who were committed to change but were confronted with massive resistance from conservative whites who wanted to keep the races separate. The boards of education in these two cities tried to walk an impossible tightrope between making progress against racial isolation and keeping the support of the white electoral majorities who were firmly against racial integration in the schools.

In Chicago the situation was quite different. The superintendent there was resistant to even symbolic gestures toward desegregation, and the civil rights organizations in town were just beginning to organize. Martin Luther King, Jr., had failed to provide much progress in civil rights for Chicago by the end of 1966. While New York and Detroit had been developing desegregation movements beginning in the late 1950s, with some sympathetic board members voicing support as the 1960s began, Chicago was late to develop any organizational or elite support for desegregation. Whereas by the mid-1960s Detroit was governed by a liberal-labor-black coalition (symbolized by the election of James Cavanaugh in 1961), and New York was also governed by a liberal reform coalition (reflected in the election of John Lindsay in 1965), Chicago's ruling coalition was constructed by a conservative political machine and run by Richard J. Daley. The Chicago School Board was resistant to even discussing desegregation, and those who favored it were unable to mobilize much elite support.

Black grassroots support for an end to school segregation was very high by 1963 in all the cities. New York and Chicago both had student boycotts in 1963 in which about half of the students stayed out of school for one day. But this enthusiasm was hard to transform into continued mass mobilization. The movements for desegregation were fragmented in all three cities, and the elite support in Detroit and New York had to contend with serious resistance from whites. Detroit made the most progress throughout the sixties in integrating the school work force and responding in other ways to the demand for racial progress.

In recent years, Detroit has recentralized its school system; the interests of black middle-class professionals have dominated the debate about schooling, while business interests have moved away from a commitment to decentralization. Our interviews reflected this trend. Rather than having radically different views of the system, Detroit insiders and outsiders had similar views of the educational leaders within the city. For example, as shown in Table 2.1, we found

Table 2.1

Detroit Ratings of School System by Insiders and Outsiders

How effective is _____ in school reform leadership?

	General Superintendent		School Board		Union	
	Insiders (%)	Outsiders (%)	Insiders (%)	Outsiders (%)	Insiders (%)	Outsiders (%)
Somewhat / Very	58	42	33	25	17	25
Not very / Not at all	33	58	49	75	75	67

Note. Insiders $n = 12$, outsiders $n = 12$. Where percentages do not add up to 100%, it is due to no answer / don't know.

that 42 percent of outsiders felt that the general superintendent was "somewhat" or "very" effective in school reform leadership, and 58 percent of insiders rated the general superintendent the same. Insiders and outsiders also had similar views of the union. Outsiders' harsher view of the board is reflective of change in board leadership during the time of our study. Business organizations were frequently mentioned by both insiders and outsiders as an important source of educational reform leadership. The combination of a liberal establishment (which emerged in the early sixties as a coalition between white liberals, the unions, and the black community) with the paternalistic attitude of the business community toward blacks set up a situation that spawned an early decentralization law but ended with the reassertion of institutional power as blacks took over the control of city hall, the teachers union, and the school bureaucracy. The incorporation of minority interests into the governance structure of the city meant that future changes would be made within the system. The movement toward enablement in Detroit is indicative of the recent shift back to institutional power.

Today New York City has an articulate white reform interest group that has worked out a modus operandi within the school bureaucracy, bureaucratizing participation and expanding the role of the community within a strong administrative environment. Historically, the reform temperament had been able to challenge entrenched interests at the polls and compete with the New York machine for control of the government. This meant that the pressure for decentralization and democracy would find its meaning within the political structure of the city. The early incorporation of minority interests sig-

Table 2.2

New York Ratings of School System by Insiders and Outsiders

How effective is _____ in school reform leadership?

	Chancellor Insiders (%)	Chancellor Outsiders (%)	School Board Insiders (%)	School Board Outsiders (%)	Union Insiders (%)	Union Outsiders (%)
Somewhat / Very	87	57	87	7	100	57
Not very / Not at all	13	29	13	93	0	43

Note. Insiders *n* = 8, outsiders *n* = 14. Where percentages do not add up to 100%, it is due to no answer / don't know.

naled that the development of decentralization would be within the schooling structure.

Our interviews suggest that outsider concerns, like decentralization, have become absorbed into the system. As shown in Table 2.2, although outsiders in New York were more critical of the system than were outsiders in Detroit, they still tended to give insiders (except for the school board) fairly good ratings. For instance, 57 percent of outsiders rated the chancellor as "somewhat" or "very" effective in school reform leadership (although 87 percent of insiders rated the chancellor as effective). Although educational reform groups are quite established in New York, they have become integrated with the system and are less critical of insiders than they were in the 1960s. The school board and chancellor are still in control, and both insiders and outsiders have similar goals for the system. Indeed, the hiring of Joseph Fernandez as superintendent in 1989, one of the key architects of the Dade County enablement strategy, suggested that empowerment and administrative control were not mutually exclusive, and that democratization could increase administrative control when administrators are skilled.

The story of Chicago is still unfolding. Perhaps in reaction to so many years of centralized control and the recalcitrance of school insiders to the calls for inclusion and dispersal, the Chicago strategy is the most dispersed and has the most politically developed set of reform organizations pursuing dispersal, with what until this point has been solid business and foundation support. The teachers union, the superintendent, and the board have all lost considerable power and legitimacy during the reform period. The result is the erosion of black

Table 2.3

Chicago Ratings of School System by Insiders and Outsiders

How effective is _____ in school reform leadership?

	General Superintendent		School Board		Union	
	Insiders (%)	Outsiders (%)	Insiders (%)	Outsiders (%)	Insiders (%)	Outsiders (%)
Somewhat / Very	33	9	67	9	83	52
Not very / Not at all	67	86	33	86	17	43

Note. Insiders *n* = 6, outsiders *n* = 21. Where percentages do not add up to 100%, it is due to no answer / don't know.

middle-class power and the emergence of white reformers as the arbiters of the new procedures, often speaking for the black poor— and this with a white mayor firmly ensconced at city hall. It is conceivable that black leadership might emerge from the ranks of the decentralized school councils, but it is hard to imagine them developing a strategy for change that would lead to redistribution.

As would be expected, outsiders in Chicago were extremely critical of the general superintendent, school board, and union prior to implementation of their most recent school reform. As shown in Table 2.3, for example, 86 percent of the outsiders rated the general superintendent and school board as "not very" or "not at all" effective in school reform leadership. The union received a higher rating by outsiders than might be expected, although the union did less to oppose reform than did the board or superintendent. Outsiders, such as educational reform organizations and the state legislature, were perceived by most of the respondents in our survey to be important actors in the reform process.

The resistance of the Chicago school system to the demands for inclusion and the repeated failure of the bureaucracy to respect, let alone respond to, the demands of local and state elites for improvement in education led to the development of a middle-class reform position outside the bureaucracy. Funded by business foundations and used as watchdogs and forums for innovation, these organizations developed the legitimacy and authority with the media and business organizations to challenge the public schools for ascendancy in setting the policy agenda in schooling. Even as the bureaucracy and board increased their minority membership to match the composition

Table 2.4

Dade County Ratings of School System by Insiders and Outsiders

How effective is _____ in school reform leadership?

	General Superintendent		School Board		Union	
	Insiders *(%)*	*Outsiders* *(%)*	*Insiders* *(%)*	*Outsiders* *(%)*	*Insiders* *(%)*	*Outsiders* *(%)*
Somewhat / Very	100	100	90	100	100	90
Not very / Not at all	0	0	10	0	0	10

Note. Insiders *n* = 10, outsiders *n* = 10. Where percentages do not add up to 100%, it is due to no answer / don't know.

of the schools, the tradition of exclusion kept the school authorities from democratizing their operation. Thus the reform impetus remained external and critical, unable to influence the school system in Chicago. This new reform overturns the tradition of exclusion, but if the experiences of New York and Detroit tell us anything, the new leadership of the system will merely learn to accommodate itself to the realities of sharing power within a bureaucracy.

The enablement cities offered a sharp contrast to the empowerment cities. In the 1980s, both Miami/Dade County and Los Angeles began internal reforms centered on dispersing control to local school sites through school-based management. Dade County carried out its plan through an impressive cooperative effort between the board of education and the teachers union. Our survey of educational elite in Dade County found no difference in how insiders and outsiders rate educational leaders in their system. As Table 2.4 shows, nearly all of our respondents, whether they were insiders or outsiders, rated the general superintendent, the school board, and the union as "somewhat" or "very" effective in school reform leadership.

The insiders have clearly controlled the educational reform process in Dade County; in fact, we found it particularly difficult to locate educational reform groups during our interviews there. When asked to name the important educational reform groups in the city, most respondents named the teachers union or board of education. Once the system took reform upon itself, the public supported the system by passing a new bond proposal. The lack of critical outside voices and the strong coalition of insiders not only resulted in an enablement policy of decentralization but also accounts for its strong support; at the time of our interviews, morale and hope were high in the system.

Although we have classified Los Angeles as an enablement city, we found less agreement between respondents there than in Dade County. Furthermore, the L.A. school system had not developed as extensive a system of school-based management as had Dade County, nor did they have the hope of large amounts of new revenues for the system. Table 2.5 shows that outsiders were more critical of insiders (e.g., 44 percent of outsiders compared to 62% of insiders rated the general superintendent as "somewhat" or "very" effective in school reform leadership) but there was little uniformity of voice among outsiders. Insiders have managed to control the reform process for decades, and outsiders have not coalesced to challenge the insiders. As in Dade County, no particular reform groups were perceived to be important in Los Angeles. These respondents reflect a political style in which insiders have maintained control by keeping outside interests dispersed. The result is an administrative decentralization similar to that in Dade County, but with less cooperation and fewer resources.

Table 2.5

Los Angeles Ratings of School System by Insiders and Outsiders

How effective is _____ in school reform leadership?

	General Superintendent		School Board		Union	
	Insiders (%)	*Outsiders (%)*	*Insiders (%)*	*Outsiders (%)*	*Insiders (%)*	*Outsiders (%)*
Somewhat / Very	62	44	75	44	88	38
Not very / Not at all	0	44	12	50	12	62

Note. Insiders $n = 8$, outsiders $n = 16$. Where percentages do not add up to 100%, it is due to no answer / don't know.

Table 2.6

Groups Named As Influential in the Reform Process

	Outsiders Mentioned (%)	*Insiders Mentioned (%)*	*Other / Missing (%)*
Enablement ($n = 148$)	36 ($n = 54$)	36 ($n = 54$)	27 ($n = 40$)
Empowerment ($n = 260$)	79 ($n = 205$)	6 ($n = 16$)	15 ($n = 39$)

Note. Only respondents who listed one or more groups in answer to the item "Name the four most important school reform groups in your city" are included in the numbers. Eight respondents from the empowerment cities and seven respondents from the enablement cities listed no groups at all. *N*s are calculated based on the number of respondents remaining times 4. "Other" includes answers such as "the media" or "the lottery." Some respondents listed only one or two groups, and their other responses would be listed under "other/missing." Outsiders include education-specific organizations, general social reform organizations, and parent groups. Insiders include teacher organizations/unions and school-system organizations (e.g., the board).

SUMMARY

In sum, we found that the following factors were key:

1. *Outsider awareness.* Outsider awareness was measured by whether outside organizations or school-system groups were mentioned more frequently as important groups for educational reform. Table 2.6 illustrates the differences between enablement and empowerment systems in terms of awareness of outsiders.

2. *Coalition.* Coalition was simply a measure of whether a prominent coalition, working toward school reform, existed in the urban area.

3. *Newer groups.* From the groups we spoke with we determined whether most outsider organizations tended to be older, entrenched groups or newer, education-specific organizations.

4. *Insiders influential.* In each urban area we asked how effective the board, union, and superintendent were in effecting school reform. This factor is also reflective of whether an insider was named as critical to passing a school reform.

5. *Importance of state legislature.* In each of our urban areas we asked whether the governor or state superintendent was important to school reform and whether any state leaders were effective players in creating reform.

Table 2.7
Factors Leading to Empowerment or Enablement

	Outsider awareness	*Coalition*	*Newer groups*	*Insiders influential*	*State legislature involved*
Chicago	X	X	X		X
New York	X	X		X	
Detroit	X	X	X		
Los Angeles			X	X	X
Dade County				X	

In our interviews, fewer outside organizations were named by respondents from enablement cities than by those in the empowerment cities. For Miami/Dade County, the level of cooperation among the union and the administration keeps outside voices from developing. For Los Angeles it seems to be more a dispersal of voices and a lack of coherence among outsiders that keeps the insiders in power. As shown in Table 2.6, we found that, unlike respondents from our empowerment cities, when respondents from enablement cities were asked to name four organizations important in school reform, the teachers union and the school board (insiders) accounted for a majority of responses.

In addition to outsider awareness, Table 2.7 illustrates whether we found the other factors to exist in each of the cities we studied. As can be seen, the factors present in Chicago reflect the existence of its most recent reform movement. Not only did our respondents consistently mention the same reform organizations, but they were also very aware of the importance of the coalition. Because of the reform movement in Chicago, half of the eight reform organizations we spoke with were newly formed education-specific groups. When respondents were asked to name someone who would be critical to passing a reform, state political leaders (such as the state speaker of the house) were mentioned most often. In chapter 5 we explore the process of reform in Chicago and how restrictions by the state legislature shaped the final reform legislation.

Although twenty years ago New York would have looked very similar to Chicago, today New York is at a different place in the empowerment process. Respondents in New York were able to name a number of outside organizations that were concerned with educational reform, but we found that, rather than outside organizations or a state legislator being key to passing a reform, the union was mentioned most often as being influential. Furthermore, the board members we spoke with did not view any particular outside organization as having influence over their decisions.

We view Detroit as passing from an empowerment to an enablement process. Of the six outsider groups we interviewed in Detroit, four were newer, education-specific groups. One of these organizations was formed to overthrow the entrenched school board and had as a goal the implementation of school-based management reforms. Although the factors in Detroit look similar to those in Chicago, we believe they indicate a movement from the empowerment control of the 1970s to a school-based enablement reform.

Los Angeles would seem to be moving toward an empowerment reform, with a number of newer, education-specific organizations and an influential state legislature. However, there was little awareness of outsider groups by the L.A. respondents in our survey, and the school system and union were mentioned most often as major educational reform organizations. The teachers union, the governor, and the state superintendent of education were believed to be critical in passing a reform. Also, as Table 2.5 illustrates, outsiders are not uniformly critical of the system.

Finally, Dade County exemplifies a system where insiders are most firmly in control. The union and the school board have worked together toward reforming the bureaucracy and, in turn, there is almost complete agreement that the system is on the road to improvement. We encountered very little criticism of the system and found it difficult to locate any outside organizations, let alone any new education-specific groups.

In the following chapters, we attempt to fill in the broad details of this analysis. We believe the cases of New York and Detroit suggest many of the inherent difficulties in an empowerment movement. The cases of Dade County and Los Angeles suggest how the institutional critique can help the system reform (as in Dade County) or how it can be used to allow organizational change but with little fundamental reform. Overall, we conclude that decentralization, especially in its empowerment form, is a poor substitute for more far-reaching reforms that fund public schools more equitably and improve the quality of education.

A recent report (McBay 1992) on the state of African Americans in this country continues to show that decentralization offers the hope of change but little else. A majority of black children are in schools with 50 percent or more minorities; one-third attend schools with 10 percent or fewer white students. McBay (1992) concludes, "The overwhelming majority of children from low-income families, including low-income African American families, will continue to attend second-rate public schools" (p. 149).

Chapter 3

New York City and Detroit: Empowerment in Perspective

Both New York City and Detroit decentralized their systems in the 1970s. Although similar in design, these two public school systems offer alternative outcomes following an empowerment model of school reform. The decentralization plans implemented in New York and Detroit consisted of elected boards for geographically determined subdistricts. These local boards, with members elected from the community, made policy for the schools in their subdistricts, leaving a district-wide board with oversight responsibilities. For both cities, school decentralization offered a way of balancing racial conflict while rebuilding legitimacy within the urban political context. The subsequent years brought different consequences for the two cities—Detroit has now recentralized after years of rancor and division, while New York has maintained its decentralized system.

In an early work on school decentralization, Scribner and O'Shea (1974) analyzed New York City's decentralization in terms of the school system's response to increased pressures from outside interests. They believed that the community pushed for control over the schools only after repeated attempts at integration led to disappointment and school achievement remained low. Scribner and O'Shea suggested that when a bureaucracy such as the school board has no effective means to "function adequately in structuring demands and supports from minority communities" (p. 391), political means of getting heard will be used. They cited a study done by Lyke (1970) that found that board members did not listen to community groups because such groups were not considered "legitimate" or representative of the entire community. Lyke's conclusion was that political parties offered the community a viable "mechanism" for communication. In turn, Scribner and O'Shea believed that decentralizing the administrative arm of the school system by allowing community groups a role in the running of the schools would improve the relationship between schools and community.

We look at New York and Detroit as examples of how inclusion in an empowerment model expands the process of school decision making but still fails to improve achievement and educational opportunities for minority students. School decentralization would not have made it into policy without the support of white conservatives and business groups. Because decentralization is inclusive—without changing resources—it was capable of drawing such broad support. In empowerment cities, reformers are often forced into trading resources for inclusion, with the hope that resources will follow. Yet once outsiders are brought into the system, the promise of change becomes a focus on governance, and that is where reformers put their efforts. In New York, the result was a melding of outsiders and insiders. In Detroit, the result was a return to recentralization and new attempts at enablement reforms.

In considering the state of these two school systems today, we conclude that decentralization did not substantially change the workings of the system. Achievement levels are low and dropout rates are high. In Detroit, the achievement for all grade levels is generally below national norms—median percentiles range from 30th to 45th for reading and 30th to 56th for math—and the dropout rate is over 41 percent (Detroit Public Schools 1989). In New York, fewer than half (46 percent) of the students read at or above grade level, just over half (58 percent) score at or above grade level on math tests (Berger 1992), and the dropout rate is over 30 percent (New York City Board of Education 1987). The student population of the Detroit public schools is almost entirely minority: Of the 180,000 students, 88 percent are black, 9 percent are white, and 2 percent are Hispanic. Of the over 900,000 students in the New York public schools, 38 percent are black, 34 percent are Hispanic, and 21 percent are white.

The general trends we recount in this chapter flesh out the factors leading toward empowerment detailed in chapters 1 and 2: the importance of an outsider coalition, conflict within the system itself, the role of state and city political leaders, and the status quo appeal of decentralization. These early stories of empowerment are meant to contrast both with the enablement systems in Los Angeles and Dade County and with empowerment in its most current form, in Chicago.

THE CONTEXT OF DESEGREGATION

Both Detroit and New York City had minority populations from the beginning of the twentieth century, but ghettos did not begin to emerge until the 1940s. Minority populations in both of these cities increased substantially with the advent of World War II; labor shortages and promises of high wages prompted a massive migration from the South. The composition of the population continued to shift as minority migration continued after the war. And as the minorities moved in, whites moved out—during the 1950s in New York, the black and Puerto Rican population increased by 770,000 while the white population decreased by 800,000 (Ravitch 1974). Similarly, between 1940 and 1950, the black population in Detroit rose over 65 percent, in contrast to white population growth of about 16 percent (Green 1974).

The growth of black migration made the issue of racial mixing in the schools more immediate. Whites living in these cities were extremely resistant to integration, especially if it was forced by government action (Taylor 1986). This posed serious problems for liberal white politicians who were brought to power by coalitions that included blacks. As outside interests increased pressure on the schools, school board officials in both cities tried unsuccessfully to manage the conflict between demands for integration and white support for segregation.

Many have argued that decentralization and its most radical form, community control, were direct offshoots of the disillusionment of community leaders and parents with the lack of integration of their schools (Gittell 1972; Scribner and O'Shea 1974). Undoubtedly, the struggles with desegregation and the role of interest representation set the political background for the movement toward decentralization. In contrast to enablement cities, where desegregation was primarily fought in the courts, in Detroit and New York the battle was a public one. The hallmark of the movement toward empowerment in these cities was widespread community involvement in desegregation; the participation and ensuing fights drew the battle lines for decentralization. In both New York and Detroit, resistance to public school desegregation forced liberal whites, labor unions, and black activists into potent political coalitions. It was through these outside coalitions that the players within the school system began to change, often through the election of liberal board members and the hiring of progressive superintendents. At the same time, black communities identified their own community leaders, which resulted in an important new force in city politics (Scribner and O'Shea 1974).

New York City

Rogers (1968) described three stages in how the school board reacted to the New York City school desegregation battle: the "academic stage," the "voluntary stage," and the "nonvoluntary stage." These stages are useful in looking at both enablement and empowerment cities, because we argue that when the system itself takes an active role in reform—that is, takes advantage of either the academic stage or the voluntary stage—then it can monitor the amount of inclusion the system will allow.

In the case of school desegregation in New York, the academic stage was from 1954 to 1960 (Rogers 1968). At this stage, the board commissioned studies and issued policy statements, but essentially maintained a "neighborhood school" ideology and continued to build schools in environments that were not conducive to integration and were zoned for housing segregation. Strikes and boycotts in 1958 and 1959 were the result of the board's failure to take any decisive steps toward integration, leading to the voluntary stage (Rogers 1968). In 1960–63, the board adopted a policy of "open enrollment" whereby students could enroll in any school throughout the district. Civil rights groups were not happy with this compromise and threatened to boycott the schools. Increased outside pressure led to the nonvoluntary stage, which was marked by the request of State Commissioner of Education James Allen, Jr., that the New York City school system submit a report on the racial composition of its schools as well as a report on their efforts toward integration (Rogers 1968). The final result of the Allen Report was that the system shifted its schools from 6–3–3 (first through sixth grade, seventh through ninth, and tenth through twelfth) to 4–4–4.

One reason the school board failed in its attempts to take decisive action toward integration was that moderate interests had a hold on the board. Traditional civil rights organizations, such as the NAACP and the Urban League, and white liberal groups, like the Anti-Defamation League and the ACLU, were all working in support of integration (Ravitch 1974; Rogers 1968). In opposition to the integration effort a number of organizations were started in both Brooklyn and Queens, and the citywide coalition against integration was called "Parents and Taxpayers" (PAT). But the centrist coalition, consisting of the United Parents Association (UPA), the UFT, the Public Education Association (PEA, an elite group composed of white professionals), and the Citizens' Committee for Children (CCC), was closely tied to the board and city officials (Rogers 1968). The centrist coalition did not wholly support desegregation and looked to compensatory programs to alleviate the problems for inner-city minority students. They represented the strong influence that white, middle- and upper-middle-class, predominantly Jewish and Protestant groups had over the school system (Rogers 1968). In essence, the centrist coalition held the balance of power between the desegregation supporters and the neighborhood school (i.e., anti-integration) advocates. Their support of a gradual approach to desegregation undermined the efforts of integrationists (Rogers 1968) and gave anti-integration groups room to grow.

The "end of school integration" (Berube and Gittell 1969) and the beginning of decentralization and community control in New York came in 1966. As directed by the Allen Report, middle schools were to open throughout the district with the purpose of having an integrated school population. The first one, Intermediate School 201 (I.S. 201) was located in Harlem (Ravitch 1974). When the creation of I.S. 201 was announced, a number of black parents and community leaders in the district formed an ad hoc parent council to get I.S. 201 integrated (Ravitch 1974). Against the group's wishes the board announced that the school would be 50 percent black and 50 percent

Puerto Rican and would have a white, Jewish principal. Their request for integration having been denied, the parent groups requested the right to control the schools, including the power to hire and fire staff (Scribner and O'Shea 1974). Feeling that their demands remained unmet, on the first day of the fall term the students and parents of I.S. 201 boycotted the school. Berube and Gittell (1969) stated, "The boycott marked the end of the school integration movement" (p. 13). There were more parent boycotts throughout the city, and the idea of community control took hold (Gittell 1972).

Unlike the desegregation process in enablement cities, the process in New York City was marked by wide community involvement. The school board and superintendent had the opportunity to take initiative for change early on, but failed to do so and were bolstered in their inaction by the moderate white middle class. The lines drawn during desegregation—civil rights groups to the Left, white liberal moderates, and white working-class conservatives—set the stage for a decentralization process that would somehow draw all groups into a compromise.

Detroit

In Detroit, the outsiders who played a significant role in both desegregation and decentralization were at the state rather than the local level. State legislators, political parties, and labor unions were the groups pushing for changes in the system. Widespread residential segregation coupled with population changes led to the involvement of both the Democratic party and labor groups in the 1960s (Glass and Sanders 1978). By 1962, black students were the majority in the Detroit public schools (LaNoue and Smith 1973). This changing pattern often meant that white children living in a neighborhood undergoing transition could be assigned to a nonwhite neighborhood school. However, as in New York, the school board instituted an open enrollment transfer policy that allowed such students to go to schools in other areas (Glass and Sanders 1978), thus preserving the segregated nature of the schools.

The 1964 Detroit school board election was one indicator of the new involvement of outside groups, as a liberal-labor-black coalition managed to put a liberal majority on the board (Grant 1971). The newly formed board chose a progressive superintendent, Norman Drachler, to begin reform of the system. At first, the board and superintendent were able to implement a number of reforms enhancing integration efforts. They hired more black teachers and appointed black administrators, rescinded the transfer policy, established more-integrative school boundaries, and used textbooks that included portrayals of blacks (Grant 1971; LaNoue and Smith 1973). These reforms did not arouse opposition in the community.

Although insiders were beginning to integrate the system, in response to the 1967 riots the state legislature began a movement toward decentralization, with little input from the school system. The desegregation process in Detroit set the stage for outsiders to make their mark on the system, and the movement toward decentralization was firmly at the state level. For both New York and Detroit, the desegregation process, with outsiders forcing the system into change, set the stage for the decentralization process.

THE DECENTRALIZATION PROCESS

Desegregation built up a conflict that would require decentralization as a compromise. In New York City and Detroit, decentralization found support with both conservatives and liberals, blacks and whites. The ability of this reform to appeal to a wide range of ideologies is key to its passage. Below, we outline the general process toward decentralization, first in New York and then in Detroit. We conclude that the governance reforms enabled the transition to a minority system that reflected rather than changed the racial landscape.

New York City

As others have noted, the decentralization movement in New York City occurred in part because there was little hope for integration. One of the obstacles to desegregation in New York was a coalition of professional groups in the school system, including teachers, principals, field superintendents, and many headquarters staff. An alignment of outside community groups—local parent associations, homeowner taxpayer and civic groups, public and private real estate interests—also helped maintain the status quo in the system. When the controversy over desegregation became intense in 1963, the "neighborhood school" ideal was used by the status quo coalition to justify segregation (Rogers 1968). Neighborhood school advocates did not want school assignments to change.

As integration failed to be implemented, desegregation advocates called for reforms that dovetailed with the neighborhood school idea: community control. They argued for deinstitutionalization, their main target being bureaucracy and professionals (Rogers and Chung 1983; Rogers 1982). Members of the Black Power movement, various student movements, and federally funded community action groups joined forces in pushing for community control of the schools. Black parents were involved; they held the school system responsible for the educational failure of their children and wanted more involvement and control over the schools their children attended (Berube and Gittell 1969; Gittell 1972). Kenneth B. Clark, a prominent scholar and supporter of desegregation, wrote that the individuals who had fought for integration were the same ones who were fighting for decentralization: "Their support for decentralization...is a strategy of despair, a strategy determined by broken promises of the White community" (Clark 1970, p. x).

Not surprisingly, as black community leadership pressed for community control (Scribner and O'Shea 1974), the idea drew support from a wide range of whites as well. This broad-based appeal was key to the implementation of community control. Foundations and universities saw it as a better way to channel black militancy, "sympathetic whites" hoped it would provide a way to improve ghetto schools through parental involvement, and conservative whites saw it as a chance to control their own schools without responsibility for black schools (Ravitch 1974). Unlike integration, which required a sharing of resources and a fundamental change in schooling, community control simply required a belief in local democracy and a condemnation of school bureaucracy.

In addition to more consensus around decentralization and community control, there was also more support from city politicians. In particular, the mayor at that time, John Lindsay, was committed to "institutional reform" (Ravitch 1974) and supported reform of the public schools. He appointed the Temporary Commission on City

Finances, which concluded that the New York schools were not getting their fair share of state education funding. At the following legislative session, Lindsay requested that the state legislature consider the New York public school system as five separate districts in order to increase funding (Ravitch 1974). The legislature's response was that the mayor would have to create a legal decentralization plan to be eligible for such funding consideration, and they offered $54 million for a plan by December of 1967 (LaNoue and Smith 1973). Such an offer spurred many community and political interests to become involved in decentralization.

The plan to decentralize evolved in a typical inclusionary fashion. Mayor Lindsay appointed an advisory panel on school decentralization. With George Bundy named as head, the panel was known as the Bundy Panel (Pellicano 1985; Ravitch 1974). When the Bundy Report was released, it suggested a far more radical decentralization than that created by the board of education. It called for the system to be organized into a federation of thirty to sixty school districts with autonomous local school boards, elected by both parents and the mayor (Mayor's Advisory Panel on Decentralization 1969). Despite coalitions in support of community control (one coalition included twenty-six civil rights and civic community groups), the plan was opposed by all the educational professional groups, which included the Council of Supervisory Association (CSA, made up of mostly school administrators), the UFT, and the board of education (Berube and Gittell 1969; Ravitch 1974; Rogers 1968). Many civil rights groups and white civic leaders opposed the plan because they still hoped for greater integration (Ravitch 1974), and some traditional white liberals thought community control was separatist (Berube 1969). In the end, the failure of all parties to agree on one plan weakened the final product—the state legislature passed neither the Bundy plan nor one of the other plans introduced by the school board or the board of regents. Instead, the legislature passed a bill that placed the issue back in the hands of the school board (Ravitch 1974).

The legislative front was not the only one where decentralization was being explored. Concomitant with the creation of the Bundy Panel, the Ford Foundation proposed three grants for experimental districts in largely Hispanic and black areas (Bresnick 1974; Pellicano 1985). In accordance with the Ford Foundation grants, the board announced the creation of three experimental districts. The districts included were I.S. 201 in Harlem, Two Bridges in the Lower East Side of Manhattan, and Ocean Hill-Brownsville in Brooklyn (Berube and Gittell 1969; Pellicano 1985; Ravitch 1974).

The development of these demonstration districts reiterates the way empowerment has been used to force reformers into an exchange of inclusion for resources. Once the districts were chosen, the superintendent decided there would be no new funds for the demonstration projects as that would defeat the experiment to discover the effects of community control (Ravitch 1974). Community groups and the union split on this issue—teachers felt the community groups should refuse to continue without additional funds, the community groups believed they could get the funds after their control was in place. The issue of resources ended the "cooperative coalition" that teachers had with the community (Ravitch 1974).

Much has been written about the experimental districts, particularly Ocean Hill-Brownsville (e.g., Berube and Gittell 1969; Gittell and Berube 1971). Ocean Hill was the site of a series of teacher strikes, where the essential question concerned the powers of the local school councils (Ravitch 1974). The governing boards felt that the board of education put too many obstacles in their path, and the board viewed the councils as advisory groups rather than policy-making entities (Ravitch 1974). Ocean Hill highlighted the difficulties in having lay control over professionals.

The State of New York finally passed a bill decentralizing the New York City school system in 1969. The bill passed with a large majority in both houses, with the deciding votes coming from the conservatives. Mayor Lindsay, such a strong supporter of decentralization early on, was largely uninvolved during this session (Ravitch 1974). The new law was opposed by many, but not all, community control advocates, because the bill dismantled the demonstration districts and failed to give complete control of the schools to the communities. Fantini wrote that the defeat of a true community control bill was a "foregone conclusion" due to the Ocean Hill teachers strikes (Fantini, Gittell, and Magat 1970, p. 155).

The Act creating the decentralized system gave responsibility for operating New York's elementary and junior high schools to the thirty-one (now thirty-two) local school boards in the decentralized districts. The bill was "at best" a compromise of various parties (Rogers and Chung 1983). Local school boards would be elected rather than appointed. The bill also created proportional representation voting for local school board members (LaNoue and Smith 1971). The act eliminated the demonstration districts and also recentralized high schools, which had just been decentralized (LaNoue and Smith 1973). The bill also strengthened the newly created chancellor position (replacing the superintendent role) and returned school board selection to the previous system whereby five members would be selected by the borough presidents and two by the mayor of New York (Bresnick 1974).

In the first election, in March 1970, only 15 percent of eligible voters voted in the election (Fantini, Gittell, and Magat 1970). Even though whites constituted only 40 percent of the population, they represented 72 percent of the new local board members (LaNoue and Smith 1971). In the 1973 elections UFT-endorsed candidates won control of most of the local boards. With the compromised decentralization plan in effect, the community control movement fell apart (Ravitch 1974).

Rogers and Chung (1983) found that decentralization worked the smoothest in the middle-class districts that originally showed the most resistance to decentralization. The areas in poverty that wanted and fought for decentralization did not have the infrastructure or necessary skills to make the best use of the authority granted under the decentralization law. Rogers and Chung also found that some of the boards took on both administrative and policy functions, while others did not. They concluded that, starting with the 1973 elections, the focus on local school councils shifted from parent-oriented candidates to those supported by the UFT, political clubs seeking patronage, parochial school groups protecting their share of federal funds, and poverty agencies also seeking patronage. The community school boards were increasingly politicized and protective of their respective groups' interests. Another pattern the authors detected was that middle-class whites were vastly overrepresented on the boards. A significant trend was the co-optation of parents by schools and the district offices.

The problems with the decentralization process that Rogers and Chung and others found in New York in the early 1970s continued into the 1980s. Today in New York there are thirty-two local school boards, which have administrative responsibility for establishing local programs, selecting textbooks and instructional materials, setting local financial priorities, and selecting supervisory staff. But the central board still controls the funding and maintenance of the schools and is also responsible for selecting the chancellor of the school system. The result of this division of labor is that both parents and school staff are unclear about their responsibilities and who is accountable for what (Wilner 1987).

A report commissioned by the PEA found that although there were positive aspects of decentralization, there were also a number of negative outcomes. Some of the negative outcomes resulted from the system for electing the community school boards. The structure of the subdistrict elections increased the politicization of the local boards. In particular, proportional voting, which was meant to give minorities full representation, was confusing to many voters (Lederman, Franckl, and Baum 1987; Manhattan Borough President's Task Force 1987). Restrictions in the decentralization law and by the central board limited the possible effects of the local boards. The PEA report and a report commissioned by the Manhattan borough president also suggested that school boards have become highly politicized, and that election turnout continues to decline. Special interest groups, including unions, churches, and political clubs, dominate local school boards (Lederman, Franckl, and Baum 1987; Manhattan Borough President's Task Force 1987). Central and local authorities have been in a continuous battle over power and turf since the decentralization law went into effect (Lederman, Franckl, and Baum 1987).

During the 1980s the proposed reforms centered on trimming the powers of the central board of education (Perlez 1988) and reforming the election of the local community school boards. The local boards were under increased scrutiny: many were investigated for improper conduct. The legislature also created the Temporary State Commission to Examine Decentralization in New York City, to be chaired by Assemblyman Serrano. The commission was directed to study and make recommendations on issues surrounding decentralization.

Detroit

Although both New York City and Detroit illustrate the importance of outside interest groups in the school reform process, the path Detroit took to decentralization was markedly different from that taken by New York. New York reformers and community members turned to decentralization after policies to integrate had failed to be implemented. In contrast, in Detroit decentralization was posed as a viable alternative to desegregation by the state legislature at the same time as the Detroit school board was designing an integration plan.

In response to the 1967 riots in Detroit, both black and white legislators filed bills during the 1968 legislative session to establish a decentralized school system. Although these bills were opposed by civic groups, school groups, and some black community members, they signaled two changes in the politics of school reform. First, the arena for decision making had clearly shifted from the Detroit school system to the Lansing legislature (LaNoue and Smith 1973). Second, decentralization's having been embraced by both black nationalists and white liberals suggested that decentralization could find the broad-based support that desegregation lacked.

In the following year, State Senator Coleman Young filed a bill to create semiautonomous regions within the Detroit school district. The school board, while supporting decentralization (Grant 1971), stayed out of the legislative debate (LaNoue and Smith 1973), as did the superintendent (Glass and Sanders 1978). The Detroit Federation of Teachers lobbied to protect teachers' rights under the bill, but did not actively oppose the bill. Meanwhile, the major outside actors, such as the NAACP, PTA, Urban League, unions, and the business community, played no role in the debate over Young's bill (LaNoue and Smith 1973). The one-page bill became law in 1969, largely due to Senator Young's support of the measure. Thus, the first round over decentralization occurred without a struggle and revealed the tendency of the state legislature to intervene in Detroit's school affairs. The Detroit school establishment, unions, and interest groups did not mobilize around the issue, nor did community or parent groups demand the imposition of community control, as had occurred in other cities, like New York.

Decentralization was of little concern to the Detroit school system, because the liberal school board still planned to pursue its goal of school integration (LaNoue and Smith 1973). To this end, they enlisted the help of the Ford Foundation in creating a desegregation plan. The eventual plan created new boundaries requiring the busing of black students to white schools and, for the first time, white students to black schools (Glass and Sanders 1978; Grant 1971). When details of the plan were leaked to the press, black and white communities went into an uproar—both wanted racially homogeneous districts (LaNoue and Smith 1973). The legislature responded by passing a new decentralization bill that had children attend the schools nearest their homes, thereby ensuring continued segregation (Dimond 1985). Meanwhile, white parents formed the Citizens' Committee for Better Education to recall the liberal school board members who had supported the original decentralization plan (Grant 1971). As in New York, community control gained support in Detroit because ideologically it appealed to those who desired to keep the races separate and those who believed in giving power to the local communities.

The new decentralization law, Act 48, created eight regions with five-member boards. The central board was expanded to include the top vote-getter from each of the regional boards and five at-large members. Boundaries would be created by a gubernatorial commission, with the stipulation that each child go to her or his neighborhood school. The commission established five black regions and three white regions (Glass and Sanders 1978). The regional boards had some power, but budgeting, labor issues, and construction decisions remained under the control of the central school board (Glass and Sanders 1978).

With the passage of Act 48, the battle lines were drawn. The national NAACP finally became interested in Detroit and filed suit to block the state's new decentralization plan and allow the original plan to take effect (Green 1974). The Urban League, teachers union, and labor supported the board's original desegregation plan (LaNoue and Smith 1973), while radical blacks, the white community, and the state legislature opposed it. Eventually, the liberal board members were recalled. New elections in the early 1970s led to victories for conservative whites and the resignation of the superintendent. As Glass and Sanders (1978) noted, "[T]he immediate effect of decentralization was the creation of racial polarization and elimination of blacks from positions of power and influence" (p. 28).

The second round over decentralization revealed the political power structure that was to dominate the Detroit public school system throughout the 1960s and 1970s. The state legislature, with the support of the white community and radical black leaders, chose community control over integration, and they had the political power to enforce their goals. The school board and superintendent discovered their lack of power concerning integration reforms. The union and reform groups such as the NAACP, Urban League, and New Detroit came to the side of the school board and superintendent, but with little noticeable effect. Locally, the mayor and other city officials avoided the controversy surrounding the schools (LaNoue and Smith 1973).

After the second decentralization bill became law, the fight over desegregation began in earnest, but it was largely a battle in the courts. The NAACP named state officials and the new school board as defendants in a suit alleging that the new decentralization law, Act 48, caused de jure segregation in Detroit (Dimond 1985). The courts agreed with the plaintiffs that local and state policies had caused residential and school segregation, and ordered the Detroit school board to create a magnet school plan within 30 days and a desegregation plan within 90 days (Green 1974). In response to white flight to the suburbs and the growth of blacks to 64 percent of the Detroit student body by 1970, the courts also ordered the state to construct a metropolitan desegregation plan for the Detroit area within 120 days (Dimond 1985). In the end, the school board failed to create a magnet school plan amenable to the courts. A two-way busing plan was enforced, and the decision was appealed.

On the first appeal, the Sixth Circuit Court of Appeals accepted the metropolitan busing plan but ordered the district court to hear the arguments of any suburban district affected by the plan (Dimond 1985). This apparent victory for the plaintiffs was only temporary. On 25 July 1974, the Supreme Court reversed the appeals court decision by a 5–4 vote and limited any desegregation attempts to the school district of Detroit. Due to the demographic makeup of the city, this ruling effectively prohibited the desegregation of the Detroit public schools and appeared to affirm the power of Michigan's political leaders and Detroit's white community. However, decentralization had altered the power structure, and the regional school board elections in 1974 resulted in a significant increase in the number of black groups represented—such as Black Parents for Quality Education, the unions, the NAACP, and the Urban League. In addition 1973 saw the election of Detroit's first black mayor, former state senator Coleman Young.

Although decentralization increased the power of the black community, it also appeared to add only another bureaucratic layer without improving the system (LaNoue and Smith 1973; Ornstein 1973). Some thought the regional boards had become a wasteful patronage system and had increased the financial problems experienced by Detroit. Beyond finances, opponents of decentralization claimed that achievement scores had dropped and that the regional boards helped obscure the issue of accountability. Parents and the community did not know whether the regional boards, central board, or superintendent should be held responsible for the declining scores. Finally, the dual result of decentralization—that blacks achieved political power, but that whites still maintained power in many areas—contributed to the dislike of decentralization.

In the late 1970s, there was a call for recentralization. According to John Elliott, president of the Detroit Federation of Teachers (DFT), the union had become an opponent of decentralization. The state legislature, though, felt that they could not mandate recentralization of the Detroit school system, especially as the author of the original decentralization bill, Coleman Young, was now mayor of Detroit. When Elliott became president of the DFT, he proposed a public referendum, and the state legislature agreed by placing Proposal S on the September 1981 election ballot in Detroit. Proposal S abolished the regional boards and returned sole authority over school issues to the central school board.

This reform effort revealed a shift in the school political power structure back to the school system. The DFT, the central school bureaucracy, and especially Superintendent Arthur Jefferson all favored recentralization. Community groups were split, with the Black Parents for Quality Education opposed to recentralization and New Detroit (a coalition composed of economic elite opposed to desegregation in the 1960s) in favor. The state legislature played a noninterventionist role, instead allowing the citizens of Detroit to decide the issue. In 1981, the public approved Proposal S by a wide margin, thus mandating the first major reorganization in fifteen years that was not instigated by the state legislature. Unlike the battles over desegregation and decentralization, this reform had been initiated by the school establishment and accepted by the community. Mayor Young and other city political leaders were not active in this battle.

The recentralization plan abolished the eight districts and created seven wards in their place. The central board was to consist of eleven members, with one elected from within each ward and four at-large members.

The economic benefits of recentralization are unclear. Some claim it saved the system $6 billion, and others argue that it resulted in no financial savings. Recentralization has not solved Detroit's academic problems either. Throughout the 1980s Detroit's dropout rate exceeded 40 percent (Detroit Public Schools 1989), and 30 percent of Detroit's high school graduates did not pass a basic skills test. In addition, longtime board members incurred the wrath of the media and public because of their use of chauffeur-driven cars and their purchase of home computers with school monies (White 1988).

The failure of the Detroit public schools and the disenchantment with the board led to a new reform movement in Detroit. During the 1988 school board elections, a reform group named HOPE campaigned on a platform that promised the creation of a solid core curriculum and the empowerment of local school communities and educators (HOPE 1988). HOPE stood for Frank *H*ayden, David *O*lmstead, and Larry *P*atrick for *E*ducation. Their plans included moving the power and responsibility for educational concepts, allocation of resources, and school environment down from the board of education to the school itself (HOPE 1988). This three-person team ran against three longtime board members and created a bitter fight with the entrenched school establishment and Mayor Young. Labor unions, the DFT, and the business community supported the HOPE team, as did the citizens of Detroit, who gave them a solid victory.

The new drive for local school empowerment revealed the stability of the political structure that was forged during the recentralization reform. The more-recent decentralization drive has emphasized local school empowerment. Though Detroit's electorate supports this concept, the school board is responsible for the reform. Different people occupy positions of power, but the relative groupings remain the same. This drive was spearheaded by the school board and union without any involvement by the state legislature. As with all the previous reforms, the citizens and reform groups of Detroit played a significant role and determined the direction of policy making in the Detroit public schools. Unlike the other reforms, this one provoked the involvement of the mayor and revealed his diminished ability to influence school policy. Finally, the reform demonstrated the power of the school board over the superintendent. Dr. Arthur Jefferson was replaced by Dr. John Porter, an educator with goals similar to those of HOPE.

With the cooperation of the DFT, school board, and new superintendent, the movement of power to a lower level is being accomplished without adding bureaucratic layers. It is more an enablement type of reform, with the school board squarely in control of devolving power. Because this reform has the support of the educational establishment and the electorate, its chances for success appear high. Detroit offers the possibility of observing how one system moves from empowerment to enablement, and the hope that an internal decision to decentralize will be more effective in improving student performance than was the external imposition of decentralization.

CONCLUSION

With the passage of time, the consequences of empowerment strategies for decentralization become clearer. In neither case has the political empowerment of the community led to the kinds of changes promised by the proponents of change. The power of institutional interests continues to dominate decision making after decentralization, and the social and economic forces that produce poor educational performance continue to influence outcomes. Both cities continue to grapple with the problems of educating children from poor families with limited resources. Changes in governance helped with problems of legitimacy while shifting the debate about urban education toward issues that seem much less central some twenty years after they were introduced.

NOTE

Some background research and writing for this chapter were done by Kristin Carman and Karen McCurdy.

Chapter 4

Creating Enablement: Dade County and Los Angeles

We have argued that decentralization is built on the rhetoric of inclusion and deinstitutionalization. Further, we have differentiated between two types of decentralization: empowerment and enablement. New York City and Detroit are early examples of empowerment, and Chicago is the most recent empowerment reform; the reformers in these systems drew their moral and political strength from the inclusionary ideal. In contrast, Miami/Dade County and Los Angeles, our enablement cases, are examples of systems that effectively mastered the deinstitutionalization critique to reform themselves from the inside.

Our analysis of school decentralization has hinged on the way cities handle the problem of racial inclusion. One important difference between enablement and empowerment cities is that neither Los Angeles nor Miami/Dade County experienced the magnitude of black migration that the other cities in our study have. Dade County's black population stands at 19 percent, while Los Angeles's is a few percentage points lower. Both cities have experienced civil unrest—L.A. in the 1960s and 1990s, and Dade County in the 1980s—but neither had the minority political development of Chicago, New York, or Detroit. Although both Dade County and L.A. have large Hispanic populations, the Hispanic interests have been much less focused on school issues than African American interests have been.

Another difference between the enablement and empowerment cities is that desegregation was not such a contentious issue; early efforts at decentralization gathered little momentum in the 1970s. Los Angeles came close to passing an empowerment decentralization plan in the late 1960s, only to have the legislation vetoed by then Governor Reagan. Since then the politics around school reform in L.A. have not revolved around decentralization. Desegregation was implemented in Dade County with little resistance, and recent decentralization plans have been a cooperative effort between the school board and the union.

Civil rights and reform organizations were weak in these cities, another factor that has resulted in enablement strategies for decentralization. Neither Los Angeles nor Dade County has broad-based coalitions with a unified demand for school reform. Similarly, in both Dade County and L.A., the school systems themselves initiated reforms and thus were able to control the direction and amount of decentralization.

In this chapter we document how school systems, in adopting the rhetoric of decentralization, are able to control the process of reform and maintain control of the system. Unlike the empowerment cities, where outside pressures ultimately led to decentralization by state mandate, enablement cities took the position of transforming themselves and in doing so were able to use decentralization to their advantage. Whereas empowerment cities are forced into a decentralization compromise, enablement cities decentralize administratively, thereby controlling the inclusionary process.

Studying the enablement cities is important in gaining an understanding of urban school reform for many reasons; chief among these is that many cities have small minority populations and strong traditions of bureaucratic politics around schooling. The power of professionals to define school reform issues has grown over the last decade, especially as the national business elite has joined the debate over educational improvement. In this environment the experiences of Los Angeles and Dade County are instructive case studies. The shifts of population to the South and West, with their traditions of nonpartisanship and "good government" styles of politics, make the enablement style the likely approach to urban school reform in the years to come.

THE ENABLEMENT CONTEXT

The Los Angeles Unified School District (LAUSD) is composed of some 825 schools with over 600,000 students, making it the second-largest school district in the nation. Over 80 percent of the students are minority—57 percent Hispanic, 18 percent black, and 8 percent Asian. Just 17 percent are white. The LAUSD has a budget of over $3.8 billion and employs 38,000 teachers, accounting for 63 percent of the educational staff. Achievement scores as measured by the California Achievement Test are low: All grade levels have a median percentile in the 30s in reading, and a median percentile range of 35th (third grade) to 50th (eleventh grade) for math (LAUSD 1988).

The Dade County public schools make up the fourth largest district in the nation, with over 250,000 students. As in Los Angeles, most of the student population (43 percent) is Hispanic, with 33 percent black (not all African American), 23 percent white, and less than 2 percent Asian or Native American. There is no official dropout rate for Dade County, but it is estimated to be about 25 percent. Achievement levels are just below the national average, with the median percentile rank on the California Achievement Test being at the 40th percentile for third, sixth, eighth, and eleventh grades. In math, the median percentile for third- and sixth-graders is above 50th, and for eighth graders it is 44th. Of the 14,000 staff members in the Dade County schools, 85 percent are teaching staff (Florida Department of Education 1988).

Perhaps due to the relatively small numbers of African American students in these school systems, neither Dade County nor Los Angeles went through long, high-profile, community-wrenching desegregation battles. Dade County, with the help of a moderate governor, was able to desegregate gradually at the local level. The fight for desegregation in Los Angeles was fought primarily in the courts, where the board of education was able to control the process. General social reform organizations, like the NAACP, marshaled little grassroots support and so were unable to gain enough attention for their cause.

Dade County

Florida's schools are organized on a county basis, with elected county school boards governing the district. Dade County includes Miami, the largest city in Florida, as well as several smaller cities and towns. Due to its urban nature—large numbers of minorities and immigrants, and a strong labor influence—the political culture of Dade County has favored liberalism, setting it apart from the rest of Florida and the South (Bendiner 1969; Dauer 1984). This culture might account for the peaceful transition to desegregation.

Under the pupil assignment laws, many school districts were able to maintain segregation legally. However, the laws also allowed school boards to make their own decisions about desegregation, and Dade County's school board took advantage of this (Cohen 1966). In this instance Dade County also benefited from the actions of a moderate governor who had appointed moderates to fill vacancies on the Dade County school board (Bendiner 1969).

The school board began its integration efforts at the junior college level, and by 1962 the segregated campuses were closed and all the students and faculty were relocated to a new, integrated facility (Cohen 1966). By the end of the first year at the new site, the faculty were given teaching assignments that supported racial mixing, and the integration of students and faculty had been achieved. Neither community groups nor the local media were apprised of the plan, so their involvement was minimal (Cohen 1966). The school board did appoint a local advisory committee to assist in the development of the junior college. As this committee did not oppose the integration plan, the board moved ahead with its agenda (Cohen 1966).

Other local actions sustained the drive toward integration. Prior to 1962, Dade County's public school teachers belonged to two racially exclusive groups. Blacks were members of the Dade County Teachers Association, while whites belonged to the Dade County Classroom Teachers Association. In 1962, the vast majority of both associations voted to merge into the Classroom Teachers Association (CTA). At the same time, the superintendent for public instruction continued his efforts toward school integration, expanding into elementary and secondary schools. By 1964, faculty integration had occurred at nineteen elementary schools and six secondary schools, while four thousand black students attended formerly all-white schools. The next year saw the appointment of a black to a high position within the school administration. Unlike in many other school districts in Florida and around the country, school integration in

Dade County was accomplished with a minimum amount of disruption or protest.

What factors led to this peaceful transition? The political culture of Dade County, along with the power of local school officials, helps to explain much of the success. As Crain (1969) discovered in his study of school boards and school integration, the political culture of a city determines the school board's response to educational reform initiatives. Cohesive boards in cities where the civic elite and electorate were progressive implemented desegregation in their schools. Dade County, with its large minority population and strong labor unions, had a political culture conducive to desegregation. By that time, some unions had begun to champion black causes across the United States. Dade County's teachers associations reflected this trend by combining into one integrated union. In addition, the electorate of Dade County (with the help of a moderate governor) chose moderate school board members, who in turn worked with a superintendent committed to gradual integration. While the state legislature and governor fought to maintain segregation, the local school officials in the county were able to integrate their schools without interference from the state. Local civil rights groups, business leaders, and community organizations did not appear to be active in this process. The decision to integrate and the power to implement that decision clearly rested with the school board and superintendent, with the support of the union.

Los Angeles

Through the 1960s and 1970s, Los Angeles, and California in general, was considered a leader in educational reform (Massell and Kirst 1985). As in other large urban school districts, the Los Angeles public school system attempted many reforms in order to increase achievement and equalize schooling. Desegregation reforms began in the 1960s and continued through the early 1980s.

Orfield (1984) noted that of all the "big cities to undergo desegregation," Los Angeles was "the first where existing desegregation was dismantled with court approval" (p. 339). The case of *Crawford v. Board of Education of Los Angeles,* a class action suit accusing the board of failure to integrate, was filed in 1963 and has had a long history in the courts (Woo 1988). In 1970, a California superior court held for the plaintiff, finding both de facto and de jure segregation. An appeal was filed, and in 1975 the California court of appeals reversed the decision. On appeal, the California Supreme Court in 1976 upheld the original ruling, but without specifying what percentages constituted desegregation, and without affirming the trial court's finding of de jure segregation.

After the board was ordered to "demonstrate meaningful progress" in desegregating (Woo 1988), a trial court-ordered plan went into effect in 1978. In 1979, however, as the trial court held hearings to assess the constitutionality of its mandatory reassignment plan, California voters approved Proposition 1, limiting state courts' power to order mandatory integration through busing. The court of appeals subsequently upheld Proposition 1, and struck down the 1978 desegregation order. An "all-voluntary" desegregation plan was submitted by the board and approved by the trial court in 1981 (Orfield 1984).

The "dismantling of desegregation," which began in December 1980, was perceived as the end of busing and desegregation in California (Orfield 1984). Although promises were made that more monies would go to poorer schools when mandatory desegregation ended, this did not happen. *Crawford v. Board of Education* pitted liberal, not-for-profit reform groups, such as the NAACP and the ACLU, against a very well-organized, well-represented, well-funded board of education. The board was more capable of using the judicial system to its advantage, which is precisely what it did in managing to take the case to the court of appeals. Furthermore, in the early 1980s the board was ruled by members who had been backed by an organization called Bus Stop, a group that originated in the San Fernando Valley for the purpose of ending mandatory integration. By helping to elect members who sided with its position, Bus Stop also influenced the board's position in the Crawford case.

In the 1970s and 1980s the Hispanic population in the schools grew to surpass that of blacks, yet Hispanics were not represented in the desegregation fight (although the Mexican American Legal Defense Fund later filed a separate suit dealing with desegregation). Little research existed on how Hispanic communities were affected by desegregation, and the Los Angeles Hispanic community was not mobilized around the issue—surveys indicated they were split on desegregation. Thus, a major portion of the persons who would be affected by the decision were neither visible nor supportive in the fight (Orfield 1984). The "reform group position," while prominent in the form of the NAACP and ACLU, lacked major grassroots community support and was not effective in forcing mandatory desegregation. The lack of community support might also have sent a message to the courts that desegregation was better left alone.

The conservative political culture of Los Angeles produced a conservative board, one that was not interested in desegregation. In his analysis, Crain (1969) distinguished between "symbolic goals" and "welfare goals" for reform groups focused on desegregation. Symbolic goals were those gained "to persuade society to accept the concept of racial equality" (p. 117). Conversely, welfare goals were those that dealt with the immediate improvement of the environment for African Americans. Crain believed that many national civil rights organizations, such as the NAACP, had symbolic goals as their mission more than welfare goals, and that this caused a split from the grassroots community. In empowerment cities, the split between the civil rights organizations and the community groups left in its wake strong community organizations that could mobilize behind decentralization. The desegregation fight in enablement cities did not have this ultimate effect. For both the L.A. and the Dade County systems, the aftermath of desegregation left strong school systems still in charge.

THE PROCESS OF ENABLEMENT

In chapter 2, we noted the lack of outsiders in enablement cities and how this contributes to the system remaining in charge. In Dade County, the union and board continue to work together on enablement-oriented reforms. This allows insiders to project a progressive attitude and give the public hope for the future. There is little if any animosity between teachers and administrators, which also promotes the idea that the insiders are willing to compromise and pull together to make improvements. Los Angeles does not have the cooperative setting of Dade County. Instead, Los Angeles has been able to neutralize outside criticism because the governor has hesitated to intervene in local matters, and because the system took sufficient inclusive action to diffuse outside community interests. In addition, constant financial crises have focused public attention on referenda rather than changes in governance, given the nonpartisan political culture.

The lack of an outsiders coalition in Dade County has left the field open for insiders to control the educational agenda. Beginning in the 1960s, statewide educational policy making was dominated by local superintendents, school board members, teachers, and the Florida Department of Education (Kimbrough, Alexander, and Wattenberger 1984; Cunningham 1978). Due to this control by the insiders, throughout most of the 1960s educational policies centered on funding, not governance (Cunningham 1978). The state legislature had relatively little influence on the content of these measures. This situation ended with the 1968 statewide teachers strike, which lasted twenty-one days, involved over thirty-five thousand teachers, and was the first statewide strike in the nation (Kimbrough, Alexander, and Wattenberger 1984).

Although the strike left the educational coalition fragmented at the state level (Kimbrough, Alexander, and Wattenberger 1984), for Dade County the strike ultimately strengthened the power of the teachers union and led to a new level of cooperation for administrators and teachers. After the strike, some Dade County teachers sued the school board and CTA on the grounds that the union had not been chosen by all the teachers as the sole bargaining agent (U.S. Department of Labor 1989). Eventually the suit reached the Florida State Supreme Court, which ordered the state legislature to enact a collective bargaining law for public employees (U.S. Department of Labor 1989). In 1974, the legislature did so. Dade County's teachers union, renamed the United Teachers of Dade (UTD), immediately filed for certification and, with the support of the Dade County School Board, received certification in 1975. As the U.S. Department of Labor (1989) noted, this action was to mark the beginning of the "formal, noncontroversial relationship between the school administration and the union, a relationship that continues today" (p. 2). According to Pat Tornillo (personal communication), executive vice president of the UTD, this law ended an era of confrontation between union and management by providing an orderly method for addressing controversial issues. Dade County's transition to collective bargaining was made smoother because the union and management had engaged in such bargaining prior to the law's passage, thereby creating a more cooperative environment.

In Los Angeles, much of the impetus for school reform has come from the courts, public referenda, and the state legislature, and there has been no unified vision of what direction reform should take. The courts have occasionally intervened, as when they decided the fate of busing in Los Angeles (Orfield 1984). The public referenda have played a huge role in shaping the system while bypassing both the legislature and the courts, as in the recent case of Proposition 98. The state legislature has often acted as a catalyst to reform in the district (LaNoue and Smith 1973), and because of state intervention California has the "longest education code in the country" (Massell and Kirst 1985, p. 124). Despite these outside pressures, the types of reforms that have been implemented in the Los Angeles public schools have often remained under the control of the district itself. Although outsiders may suggest the direction of reform, the insiders clearly control the shape and input of the reforms.

In the following sections, we turn to how insiders have utilized inclusion in Dade County and Los Angeles. As with all movements toward decentralization, the state legislature played some role in both Dade County and Los Angeles. But unlike the empowerment cities, where state legislatures were strong enough to put through radical decentralization packages, neither Dade County nor L.A. was forced in that direction. In both cases, the political culture that shaped desegregation also formed the approach to decentralization.

Dade County

After the teachers strike in 1968, the newly established trust between the union and school administration in Dade County met its first test in response to the state legislature's first poststrike reform initiative. In 1971, Governor Reubin Askew established the Citizens' Committee on Education, which consisted of legislators, business and industry representatives, professionals, and academics. The committee's recommendations resulted in the passage of the Florida Educational Finance Program (FEFP) in 1972 (Kimbrough, Alexander, and Wattenberger 1984). According to Gerald O. Dreyfuss, deputy superintendent of schools, this law reallocated education money so that each school received funds it could allocate as it saw fit. The law also created school advisory councils for each school to assist in decision making by providing community input to school authorities (Kimbrough, Alexander, and Wattenberger 1984). Finally, the law gave increased power over curriculum decisions to local school officials. All these provisions resulted in the creation of a decentralized educational process known as "school-based management."

As described by Cunningham (1978), FEFP only had the support of the governor and the state legislature. Almost every educational group and leader opposed the law's concept of school-based management. The state school board association and the superintendents' association actively opposed the bill on the grounds that the law would not be compatible with collective bargaining and would diminish their power. The major teacher associations also fought the bill, fearing that teachers would lose rights and autonomy. Finally, the statewide PTA came out against the bill because of its conflict with the powers and goals of the local PTAs.

In Dade County, the UTD did not endorse school-based management (Cunningham 1978), nor did it receive the backing of parents or the business community. The school board was split on the issue. Finally, the superintendent, who had attempted a pilot project with school-based management, ended it. Thus, even though the state legislature, governor, and local superintendent favored school-based management, opposition by the union, discord among school board members, and lack of support by parents and business ended Dade County's first experiment with school-based management. Once again, the state was unable to impose its educational priorities on the Dade County public school system.

The key to Dade County's ability to fight a state mandate was improved relations between the union and the school administration. In the 1970s, the first formal contract established union-management task forces to address issues not covered by the collective bargaining agreement, and the second contract instituted faculty councils at each school (U.S. Department of Labor 1989). The councils, consisting of principals and elected teachers, functioned as advisory bodies to local school officials. These first contracts helped establish a nonadversarial working climate in the Dade County public schools.

In 1985, the union and superintendent created the Joint Task Force on the Professionalization of Teaching, cochaired by Pat Tornillo and the superintendent of schools, Leonard Britton (U.S. Department of Labor 1989). This task force used the deinstitutional- ization critique to reform themselves. According to Tornillo, he and Britton agreed that a business-as-usual attitude would not improve the schools. Both the teachers union and the board agreed that the schools were not making significant progress in achievement scores, dropout rates, and other vital areas. In addition, the public appeared unhappy with the current system of public education, and both the union and the school system feared a mass movement toward support of a voucher system or tuition credit plan. On the national level, *A Nation at Risk,* the Carnegie Report, and other educational research encouraged a restructuring of the school system with an emphasis on improving the teaching profession. The joint task force was designed to study these issues and make recommendations for change.

The outcome of this collaboration was the creation of a school-based management/shared decision-making (SBM/SDM) pilot project around 1986. The project restructured the system by giving control over decisions to local schools (Cistone, Fernandez, and Tornillo 1989). Under this system, school authorities have control over the discretionary budget, curriculum, and personnel issues. While no additional funds were to go to schools in the pilot, these schools were promised support from the board and union in obtaining waivers from union contracts and school board policies or Department of Education regulations necessary for implementing SBM/SDM in the school (U.S. Department of Labor 1989).

The first year of the project involved planning and proposal development. To promote interest in the pilot project, Tornillo and Britton spoke at several schools throughout the 279-school system. An acceptable proposal had to be endorsed by two-thirds of the faculty, utilize school-based budgeting software, define the proposed shared decision-making process, and positively affect the educational processes at the school. Fifty-three schools submitted proposals to a ten-member task force of teachers, management and union representatives. Of these, thirty-three were accepted and about one hundred waivers were granted (U.S. Department of Labor 1989).

Implementation began during the 1987–88 school year. There were plans to have the project evaluated by the school district and by independent researchers at the University of Florida and Florida International University at the end of the 1989–90 school year. The evaluations would focus on quantitative data, such as test scores and attendance rates for students and teachers, along with qualitative data, consisting of personal evaluations by teachers, principals, and other participants in the project. At the time of our data collection in Dade County, these evaluations had not yet been conducted, but the pilot was termed a success in 1989, and plans were made to add another fifty schools to the project in the 1989–90 school year (U.S. Department of Labor 1989).

The decision to implement SBM/SDM was a complete reversal of the 1975 decision to end the school-based management experiment. In interviews, both Britton and Tornillo credited this reversal to a change in attitude on the part of the union. According to Tornillo, the union had realized that concentrating on bread-and-butter issues alone would not improve the teaching profession. A more crucial issue was whether to trust teachers and principals to make decisions regarding children's education. To give such power to the local schools required sacrifices on all sides. The superintendent and school board had to give up centralized control, while the union and its local stewards had to accept contract waivers for provisions they had fought to obtain. Assistant Superintendent Dreyfuss stated that principals and teachers had opposed the establishment of school-based management in 1975 because they had been left out of Governor Askew's 1971 task force. Since that time, the union had become a more powerful educational actor. Dreyfuss contended that the UTD had come to understand that the best way to professionalize teaching is by working with management in policy making.

One key factor in creating SBM/SDM was the improvement in union-management relations. A primary reason for the cooperation was the consistency in the cast of prominent educational leaders (Wohlstetter and McCurdy 1991). Over the past two decades, the school board has had little turnover, and the union has had the same leadership since the 1960s. The superintendent position also demonstrated continuity within the system—Superintendent Leonard Britton was succeeded by Joseph Fernandez, the former deputy superintendent of schools in Dade County. As deputy superintendent, Fernandez had shown his commitment to SBM/SDM, so his selection as superintendent in 1987 ensured the continuation of teacher professionalization efforts.

The impetus for SBM/SDM came from the union-management task force with the support of the school board. Though the initial idea for this form of decentralization came from Governor Askew's task force and the 1973 FEFP legislation, actual implementation occurred solely through the efforts of local school officials. Most of the resistance to SBM/SDM came from middle-management and some upper-management personnel who feared a loss of power and/or jobs. So far, the middle-management ranks have not been reduced. Potential educational reformers outside of the Dade County school system, such as parent, business, and community groups, have not been active in this reform effort. At the state level, the legislature continued to encourage decision making at the local school site, thereby assisting the reform effort in Dade County. However, the governor, state superintendent, and other state educational leaders did not directly influence the decision to initiate school-based management.

Los Angeles

LAUSD began decentralization efforts in 1961, before the issue of desegregation had been settled. At that time, a number of studies suggested that "greater responsiveness and efficiency" could be created in the district through some form of administrative decentralization (LaNoue and Smith 1973). Throughout the 1960s, measures were taken to decentralize, beginning with school advisory committees and gradually growing to include community representation in the creation of school curricula (through the Miller Education Act of 1968) and local school control over some discretionary budget items.

O'Shea (1975) observed that decentralization efforts in Los Angeles were primarily changes in "organizational processes, directed by school district administrators." Although pressure from minority groups forced the school district to undertake some form of decentralization, it was not the community control model favored by minorities. The year 1967 marked a turning point in the debate over community control, when it was discovered that first-, second-, and third-graders in Los Angeles scored among the lowest in the nation and that these scores reflected the poor achievement in the "inner-city, minority schools" (O'Shea 1975). Blacks mobilized first, requesting that white principals be replaced by blacks; unrest in the Hispanic community followed in 1968. As O'Shea viewed it, complying with some of the demands of the minority groups was a way for board members to disengage themselves from desegregation, something they did not wish to support. It was also at this point that the administration realized the importance of minority groups in the running of the district.

The board actively responded to the minority community, imposing administrative decentralization into twelve areas and elected school advisory councils for each of those areas. The board also directed and controlled community input through the advisory councils and a number of minority "commissions." The first commission to be established was the Mexican American Commission, which was created during an upset over the firing of an Hispanic principal. During this struggle, the board realized it had few communication ties with the Mexican American population, and the Commission was born (O'Shea 1975). Asian American and Black American Commissions followed, but to date the Mexican American Commission appears to be the most organized and vocal (C. Barron, personal communication 1988).

Threats by the state legislature ultimately spurred LAUSD into action. In response to growing "community unrest" (Scribner and O'Shea 1974), three different bills on decentralization made their way into the legislature: the Greene bill, which specified separate school districts in the lower-achieving inner-city schools; the Ralph bill, which called for low-achieving schools in the ghettos to become "self-determination" schools run by their own councils; and the Harmer bill, which proposed breaking up the system into smaller districts (LaNoue and Smith 1973; O'Shea 1975). None of these bills received the support it needed, and the result was the creation in 1970 of a joint Committee on Reorganization of Large Urban Unified School Districts. State Senator Harmer was named as chairman and Assemblyman Greene as vice chairman, thus bringing the forces of conservative Republicans (Harmer) and liberal, minority Democrats (Greene) together. Eventually, the committee proposed the Harmer-

Greene bill, which required that the Los Angeles School Board be disbanded, twelve districts be created, and a representative from each district be placed on a central governing board (O'Shea 1975). The bill passed in both the assembly and the senate of the state legislature, but it was vetoed by Governor Ronald Reagan in September 1970 (LaNoue and Smith 1973).

At the same time as deliberations were taking place in the state legislature, LAUSD commissioned its own study and created its own task force on decentralization. Just prior to the Harmer-Greene bill, the district implemented a program to divide the district into four regions, which was followed by division into twelve regions the following year. Because the district had made these efforts toward decentralization, Reagan chose to veto the Harmer-Greene bill (O'Shea 1975). In 1971 another bill passed in the legislature, calling for the election of local school councils, but this again was vetoed by Reagan on the grounds that the district was making an attempt at decentralization and that the state should not interfere.

The district's perceived "support" of decentralization was key in keeping the legislature's initiatives at bay. And the district, through administrative decentralization, diffused the voices calling for community control. Decentralization served the additional purpose of redirecting the interest of the NAACP and other minority groups away from desegregation to achievement issues and the quality of education (LaNoue and Smith 1973). The district made a final effort to account for the public's interest in community control through a large-scale survey from which a "plan would emerge with a broad base of support" (LaNoue and Smith 1973). The sticky issues remained the same as before: changing the board structure and deciding how parents should be involved in local schools. The board finally chose to keep the current seven-member board elected at large (although in 1978 Proposition M passed, requiring that the board be elected by district) and to allow committees at each school to decide on the kind of "school-community advisory committee" they wanted (LaNoue and Smith 1973).

This plan was fine for parents in the white, better-achieving schools, but parents in the inner-city, minority, lower-achieving schools did not find in it the control or change they wanted. It is interesting to note that when decentralization was first implemented,

Caughey and Caughey (1969) suggested that it was for the purpose of maintaining segregation and decreasing equal opportunity. This same argument could be applied to the programs of decentralization enacted in the 1970s: They benefited the wealthier white districts rather than aiding the poorer minority ones.

CURRENT REFORM

Although both Dade County and Los Angeles were able to control the amount of inclusion in their systems, they differ considerably in how enablement has played out. The extensive internal reforms attempted on the part of Dade County have legitimized the receipt of additional funding. In contrast, although outsiders have still remained dispersed in Los Angeles, insiders have done little to fundamentally change the system. Los Angeles, along with all California schools, will continue to face the real possibility of a voucher system.

Dade County

Dade County's school-based management has been widely hailed as an innovative reform, and yet enrollment in Dade County schools increased by fifty thousand students over a three-year period due to refugees and immigrants (Schmalz 1989). The cost to the system includes overcrowded classrooms, lack of materials, dilapidated buildings, and a shortage of teachers. In addition, educating an immigrant child costs $3,900 per year, while the same education can be provided to a nonimmigrant for $2,600.

All these factors pointed to the need for new money to help Dade County's $1.2 billion annual budget (U.S. Department of Labor 1989) keep pace with the growing student population. The board again took the initiative and proposed to sell $980 million in school bonds for construction and renovation. Such a bond issue had to be approved with a voter referendum by the residents of Dade County. The bond referendum received a 53 percent majority in March 1988. With the support of the teachers union, Dade County PTA, and local business leaders, the board was able to convince the public of the need for this money. The $980 million was earmarked for building 49 new schools, additions at 161 current schools, and renovations at the remaining schools.

Parents, businesses, and community groups were not active in the school restructuring process, but their support for the bond issue, along with their repeated decision to reelect the same school board members, seems to indicate support of the reforms undertaken by the Dade County school system. In Dade County, major educational reform initiatives have arisen from the interaction between the union, the school board, and the superintendent, and not through outside pressure from either local or state figures. Dade County's experience with decentralization exemplifies this political power structure. The first attempt at implementing school-based management there was abandoned due to lack of local support, even though such a restructuring was mandated by the state legislature. The current decentralization experiment continues to expand, as it has the support of the county school system. By trying to create a cross-sectional, representative sample of schools and conducting independent evaluations, the Dade public schools hope to serve as a model for other large city school systems. Even without these evaluations, however, the Dade County experience should enlighten other cities to the benefits of a system where union and management define a goal and work together to achieve it.

Los Angeles

Along with the debate about decentralization and desegregation, other reforms, mainly financial, affected how Los Angeles approached questions of inequality. Eventually these overshadowed the debate on decentralization. In 1971 the case of *Serrano v. Priest* held that schools were not being funded equally. The Serrano case led to a ruling by the state supreme court that forced legislators to equalize funding across all districts (e.g., Senate Bill 90, 1972; S.B. 65, 1977). Though they did not deal specifically with education, two other financial reforms—Proposition 13 and Proposition 4—limited the funding of schools in California. Before Proposition 13, local taxes provided 70 percent of school funding. In 1978 Proposition 13 was implemented and property taxes were cut by 60 percent, which nullified earlier attempts (such as *Serrano*) at equalizing funding for all schools. In attempting to get more monies to the schools, the California state legislature approved S.B. 154 and S.B. 8, which increased state funding of the schools (Massell and Kirst 1985). Eventually schools were funded 80 percent by the state government and just 20 percent from local taxes. It was during the 1980s that many programs were cut from the schools.

After Proposition 13, the public decided to limit government spending with Proposition 4, which passed in 1978. Proposition 4 prohibited government spending from growing faster than the rate of inflation. Education, which makes up 40 percent of the state budget, was hard hit by this limit. Luddy (1988) noted that over the past decade "the percentage of personal income spent on education [in California] has declined from 4.6 percent to 3.3 percent," resulting in a "loss of $1,000 per student, per year" (p. 10). Although a case had been taken to the California Supreme Court arguing that the state's means of funding the schools was unconstitutional, it was not upheld in the courts. This 1983 decision forced educators and legislators to turn attention toward issues of reform rather than funding.

Thus, after the wave of financial reforms, in 1983 a 214-page education reform bill, Senate Bill 813, passed in the state legislature, putting into effect a number of programs and acting as a way of moving more monies from the state to local districts. As Odden and Marsh (1988) stated, "S.B. 813 spells out neither a philosophy of reform nor a cohesive strategy for changing the schools" (p. 593). What S.B. 813 did do was set out a number of policies and programs designed to change, with one blow, curriculum, teacher incentives, graduation requirements, and other areas of education (Odden and Marsh 1988). The reform was created by Senate Education Chair Gary Hart and Assembly Education Chair Teresa Hughes, with support from State Superintendent Honig. It was also supported by the business community and community groups, with United Teachers of Los Angeles playing a part in shaping the mentor teacher portion of the bill.

The Southern California Policy Analysis for California Education Center (PACE) undertook a study to determine how successful S.B. 813 was in affecting student achievement. They found that most schools in their study enacted some portion of S.B. 813, and that there was some improvement in scores at a statewide level (Odden and

Marsh 1988). However, it was also found that students who needed extra resources did not receive an amount that would make a significant difference. Although S.B. 813 might have been widely touted in its first years of implementation, without increased funding of the schools, few of the programs mandated under S.B. 813 could be supported (M. Shrager, personal communication 1988).

After S.B. 813, reforms in the state legislature focused primarily on specialized groups such as dropouts or at-risk students. None of these reforms seems very prominent at the city level, though S.B. 813 is often mentioned as the last "educational reform" by city educators. However, outside of the state legislature, a few other reforms were subsequently initiated by the public. One was the lottery, which was approved by voters in 1984 as a way of raising money for the schools. The lottery makes up about 4 percent of the LAUSD budget, or about $183 per student. But perhaps the most significant was Proposition 98, another referendum focused on increased funding for the schools.

Proposition 98 passed in November 1988. Teachers (led primarily by the California State Teachers Association), the PTA, and State Superintendent Honig all played significant roles in its passage. Proposition 98 amended the state constitution to create a minimum level of funding for elementary and secondary schools and junior colleges. It also specified that most unspent resources would go toward education rather than be refunded to taxpayers. Governor Deukmejian and the California Taxpayers Association strongly opposed the reform on the grounds that the schools already received priority funding in California. Proposition 98 passed by a narrow margin—just over 51 percent of the 9.5 million votes. It derived its primary support in Los Angeles, where most minority and educational reform groups were in favor of it. For the 1989–90 school year, it meant a 12.5 percent increase in state funds (Snider 1989).

Apart from state propositions, LAUSD continues to implement internal reforms. Year-round schools were instituted in the mid-1980s as a solution to overcrowding in a few select schools. However, this policy has resulted in charges of racism due to the fact that most of the schools affected are minority schools. Pressure from black groups, such as the Black Leadership Coalition, which is made up of many different organizations, resulted in a pilot project called the "Ten Schools Project" (TSP). The purpose was to place the best teachers and the best resources into ten of the lowest-achieving schools in the district to see what improvements could be made (F. Haywood, personal communication 1988). The program, initiated in 1986, suffered from poor planning and disagreements between blacks and Hispanics over how monies should be used. As a result, although it is still being implemented, few positive things have been heard about the project.

One of the most recent internal reforms initiated by the general superintendent's office was called "Priorities for Education: Designs for Excellence" (PEDE). It involved evaluation by every department governed by the board and committees on a dozen or more areas, from curriculum to finance. Recommendations from these committees were compiled into a report, which was then reviewed and evaluated by administrators, teachers, parents, and students. Out of this process priorities were set for educational reform.

In May 1989, the UTLA went on strike, asking primarily for increased pay but also for more power in school governance. Superintendent Leonard Britton had just been hired in 1988 from the Dade County, Florida, public schools because of the school-based management programs implemented there, and hopes were high that he would enact similar reforms in Los Angeles. A small amount of money had been allocated in 1988 for school-based management programs, but it worked out to just $500 per school. After the UTLA strike, the settlement created locally elected boards at each school, composed of school staff, community members, and parents. These councils are made up of six to sixteen members (dependent upon school size), with half of the members on any council being teachers. In the 1989–90 school year, over two thousand parents and community members were elected, though problems such as low turnout and ballot improprieties did arise in the election process.

In this "shared decision-making" reform, the council responsibilities in the first year were limited to implementing staff development programs, creating student discipline codes, scheduling final exams and other special tests, guidelines for school equipment use, and allocation of certain discretionary monies. These responsibilities were to be altered when school-based management began in the 1990–91 school year. A "central council" composed of twenty-four members—

half appointed by the UTLA, and half by the board and superintendent—was to oversee training and monitor the local councils throughout the district.

Thus, as in other urban areas, the current state of decentralization
in Los Angeles is beginning to change. Parental participation and
community control, which were a focus of decentralization efforts in
the 1970s, are again beginning to gain importance. Though there are
many community groups involved in educational reform in Los Angeles, outside of mobilizing around a financial reform such as Proposition 98 there does not appear to be broad-based support for any one
educational reform. The business community is getting more involved
and, through the California Roundtable, has been considering other
state educational reforms. Perhaps, as O'Shea (1975) has suggested,
the ability of the Los Angeles board to change organizational processes is effective enough to keep other forces in check and to keep the
board in power. Alternatively, the huge number of immigrants making up the constituency of the district—eighty-one different languages
are present in the schools (Nazario 1989)—indicates that many parents are unable to mobilize around educational reforms, thus diffusing
community group power.

CONCLUSION

This analysis of Dade County and Los Angeles touches only briefly
on the complex reform processes in these two systems, but it does
illustrate how insiders can use the inclusionary ideal and the deinstitutionalization critique to maintain power in the system. In Dade County, there seems to be a common belief in the system and the reforms
that are being enacted. The system has been able to maintain a certain
degree of centralized control, mostly by directing the kind of decentralization reform being implemented in the schools. Furthermore, the
reform in Dade County appears to be genuinely successful, with a
shift in resources to the classroom: 85 percent of staff are teaching
staff, in comparison to other systems where teaching staff make up
just 60 percent of school personnel. Finally, improved public perception facilitated a push for new revenue. Perhaps if the school board
and superintendent had not had the foresight to work together toward

reform, there would be less power for the insiders and more power placed on the outside.

In contrast, the insiders in Los Angeles are able to control the system, not through cooperation, but through the ability to enact their own reforms, which included outsiders in the process. And with the educational reform process generally dominated by state referenda and propositions, outside interests move from proposition to proposition and leave implementation in the hands of the system.

NOTE

The initial research and writing of the Dade County portion of this chapter were done by Karen McCurdy.

Chapter 5

Chicago Overview: Empowerment Today

The Chicago public schools are responsible for educating over four hundred thousand children each year (Chicago Panel on Public School Policy and Finance 1990). They constitute the third-largest school district in the nation, with an annual budget of over $2.3 billion, over one-half of which is spent on teacher salaries and pensions (Chicago Panel 1991). Eighty percent of the students in the district are low-income. The student population is 60 percent African American, 25 percent Hispanic, 12 percent white, and 3 percent Asian/other. On national standardized tests, Chicago students rank in the bottom half of the country (Brodt 1988; Chicago Panel 1990).

The Chicago School Reform Act passed the Illinois General Assembly in 1988 (Senate Bill 1840, Public Act 85-1418) and was implemented in Chicago's complex school system the following year. Although this reform encompasses more than community control of the schools, the most radical aspect of the law is that school governance is turned over to a council at each school, composed primarily of parents and community members. One local newspaper termed it "school revolt," because the potential for change in the bureaucratic power structure was so significant (Levinsohn 1989); many researchers have also commented on the radical nature of this reform (e.g., Elmore 1991; Katz 1992).

In chapter 2 we found that many of the factors LaNoue and Smith (1973) and Boyd and O'Shea (1975) cited as producing decentralization were in place in Chicago. Low achievement, protests against the school system, outside coalitions of interest—all of these were present in Chicago. And, as was clear from the findings of our survey of educational elite, the board, superintendent, and union were believed to have little ability or power to change the system.

In the following four chapters, we trace the development of this current wave of decentralization in Chicago to show how an empowerment design was made into law. We describe how the movement toward reform in Chicago enhanced and supplemented popular sovereignty without displacing it, primarily by creating a bureaucratically limited mechanism for participation that allowed for local creativity while leaving powerful institutional actors a great deal of latitude. We outline how factors within the system and at the local school and individual levels serve to reinforce the status quo by changing processes and attitudes rather than actual school outcomes. This chapter begins with a brief summary of the struggle over desegregation, and then moves to an analysis of the 1988 Chicago school reform.

DESEGREGATION OF CHICAGO SCHOOLS

The story of school desegregation in Chicago reflects the tight control the white civic elite held over the political culture and the desire of the board to keep the schools segregated. In the 1950s, although de facto segregation was widespread due to a combination of housing practices and a strict "neighborhood school" policy, the Chicago School Board believed it had no responsibilities to desegregate (Anderson and Pickering 1986). The board interpreted the decision in *Brown* as requiring it to avoid only statutorily created segregation. And although many believed that the overcrowding in Chicago's black schools stemmed from segregation, the board and superintendent interpreted the overcrowding as due to changing city demographics rather than racial gerrymandering or segregation.

As of the 1961–62 school year, the board continued to assert that the overcrowding in black schools stemmed from innocent demographic changes and not racially motivated school boundary-line drawing (Anderson and Pickering 1986). The board attacked those who asserted that segregation was the issue and reaffirmed its resolute denial of any duty to actively integrate the Chicago schools. Instead, mobile classrooms, nicknamed "Willis Wagons" (after Superintendent Ben Willis) were dispatched to schools suffering from what the board described as "inexplicable overcrowding" (Anderson and Pickering 1986, p. 349).

The Willis Wagons served as an important symbol for those seeking to desegregate Chicago's schools. First, they stood for the board's interpretation of the cause of the overcrowding in the black schools. Second, according to Anderson and Pickering (1986), the wagons likened Willis's position to an urban version of Governor Wallace's stance in front of the schoolhouse door denying black students entry. Finally, the wagons represented the board's lack of commitment to stabilizing the racial composition in Chicago. As Peterson (1976) stated, "[P]ut more harshly—the school board wanted to discourage blacks from entering, [and] whites from leaving Chicago as a place of residence" (p. 173).

Two studies in the 1960s influenced the Chicago situation. First, the Havighurst Report, released in November 1963, found a relationship between SES and academic achievement. The report recommended that resources should be directed toward early childhood development programs and suggested $50 million in additional funding. The second study, the Hauser Report, was released in March 1964. The Hauser Report supported the claim made by many reformers and civil rights leaders that many seats in white schools were empty while black schools struggled with severe overcrowding. These statistics appeared to contradict the board's assertions and undermined its actions. Many desegregation reformers suggested that, rather than create more space in the form of mobile homes to relieve overcrowding, the board should transfer black students from overcrowded black schools to underutilized white schools.

The board, induced by the Hauser Report findings, tentatively explored possible integration techniques. It proposed a plan that would have resulted in the transfer of approximately twenty black honor students from severely overcrowded black schools to Bogan High School, an underutilized white school located on Chicago's South Side. Superintendent Willis argued vehemently against the board's proposal and threatened to resign if it passed. In addition to Willis, many white parents and community leaders objected to the board's proposal, and a vocal group of Bogan High School parents forced the board to back down (Anderson and Pickering 1986).

In other cities, like New York, the intervening factor in changing the pattern of school segregation was the progressive attitude of the city and state political and civic elite. But in Chicago, the elite, led by Mayor Richard J. Daley, supported the board of education and drew together to resist any intrusion into the board's professional assessment and discretion regarding the schools. The board was able to ignore demands by civil rights groups in part because the city elite allowed it. In fact, in 1963 Mayor Daley's blatant support of Superintendent Willis and his segregationist position led to a massive school boycott with over two hundred thousand students staying home (Lemann 1991).

Even federal intervention could not overcome the strength of the machine politics in Chicago. In 1965, the Coordinating Council of Community Organizations filed a formal complaint with the U.S. Office of Education. In its complaint, the CCCO sought to enjoin the federal government from distributing funds to the Chicago Board of Education based on the board's Title VI violations. Following the filing of the CCCO's formal complaint, the U.S. Department of Health, Education, and Welfare (HEW) began investigating the Chicago public school system. After an initial investigation, U.S. Education Commissioner Francis Keppel informed Chicago school officials that the city was in "probable noncompliance" of Title VI regulations. The HEW's finding jeopardized at least $32 million in federal funds for Chicago schools. The city's reaction to the HEW action was immediate. Mayor Daley quietly met with President Johnson in New York City. In their meeting, Daley argued that HEW's findings with respect to the city's schools and segregation were ambiguous and that, in any event, the ambiguities would be quickly cleared up. Further, Daley suggested that the city and the school board were in the best position to run the schools. President Johnson agreed and quickly diverted Commissioner Keppel from further investigation (Anderson and Pickering 1986).

Following Johnson's intervention on Daley's behalf, the U.S. Office of Education's investigation of the Chicago school system lagged. After two years of negotiations, HEW and the city entered into an agreement that resulted in the transfer of a small number of students in only one section of the city. And, by 1968, Chicago had solidified its position so that HEW no longer reviewed the Chicago school situation. Chicago also showed other cities "that civil rights enforcement could be opposed successfully through political means" (Anderson and Pickering 1986, p. 181). In fact, HEW's attempt to enforce Title VI regulations in Chicago's public school system marked a turning point in HEW's enforcement activities. Following its involvement with Chicago, HEW retreated from Northern school district desegregation enforcement.

Another difference between Chicago and other cities in gaining school desegregation was that civil rights organizations chose to focus on issues other than school integration. In the late 1960s Chicago was the site for the "civil rights movement in the North" (Lemann 1991, p. 325). Although school desegregation was the initial issue of protest, the reformers decided that "End Slums" would be a better campaign. The end result was that Daley held a series of summits in which he hammered out an agreement with Martin Luther King, Jr., where King agreed to stop protest marches and Daley agreed to an "open-housing plan" (Lemann 1991, p. 239). As Lemann put it, "Almost the instant that the summit agreement was signed...the interracial, non-violent civil rights movement in Chicago disappeared. The furtherance of black progress became essentially a black cause" (p. 240).

Throughout the 1970s, the schools remained segregated. It was not until the 1980s that desegregation efforts again surfaced. Despite HEW's failure to affect segregation in Chicago's public schools, the U.S. Department of Justice began an investigation. In 1980, the City of Chicago and the federal government entered into a consent decree that called for the board of education to file a desegregation plan by March 1981 and to implement its plan by September 1981. The board failed to meet either deadline. Instead, it submitted to the court a statement of principles and postponed compliance until 1983. In January 1983, a federal district court approved the board's desegregation plan. Pursuant to the plan, any school with up to 70 percent white students was defined as integrated. In addition, the plan called for voluntary rather than mandatory desegregation techniques. Not surprisingly, the board's plan left 58 percent of Chicago's public schools segregated.

THE DECENTRALIZATION MOVEMENT

Both Hess (1991) and O'Connell (1991) have written detailed accounts of the road to school reform in Chicago. From Hess's view as a participant observer (he is executive director of the Chicago Panel on Public School Policy and Finance, a watchdog organization of the public schools), Hess chronicles the turn in public sentiment against the schools and the creation of this radical decentralization policy. It is not our intent to rewrite the story of Chicago school reform. Instead, we focus on the factors that allowed this type of empowerment policy to take hold and the possible consequences of such a policy.[1]

In their study of the civil rights movement in Chicago, Anderson and Pickering (1986) argued that Chicago's "civic credo" helped overcome the reformers' demands for increased civil rights and desegregation. With respect to race relations in general, and school desegregation in particular, the civic credo in Chicago stood for a belief in existing social, economic, and political institutions. Those who established and maintained this credo—business, civic, and social leaders—thought that with time the existing institutions would fulfill the promise of equality. In such an environment, machine politics prevailed. In the 1960s, those who challenged the civic credo—reformers, civil rights activists, and some school board members—were viewed as irrational, obstructionist, and a threat to civil order (Anderson and Pickering 1986, p. 325).

Machine politics controlled the Chicago scene until the 1980s, when Harold Washington was elected mayor in 1983. As Chicago's first African American mayor, his election signaled the waning of machine politics and the rejuvenation of reform efforts. Although Mayor Washington did not initially focus on educational reform, he did call an "educational summit" that drew together various players throughout the city to discuss education. The summit ended up as a two-part process. Summit I, held on 21 October 1986, involved approximately thirty-five business, education, civic, and community leaders. The agenda was directed toward exploring and developing working agreements that would link education and the Chicago public school system to employment.

In September 1987 the Chicago Teachers Union (CTU) voted to strike for wage and benefit considerations. The CTU strike, lasting nineteen days, delayed the opening of the 1987–88 school year by three weeks. It was formally settled on 3 October 1987. The growing dissatisfaction with the board of education's ability to meet the educational needs of the city was galvanized by the teachers strike.

The strike mobilized a variety of community, business, and advocacy organizations to reform the school system. A meeting was called at Chicago's Loyola University in which Warren Bacon, chairman of a group of businessmen, Chicago United, gave an impassioned appeal for change. School reform groups that had been fighting the board of education for years, such as Designs for Change and the Chicago Panel on Public School Policy and Finance, headed up the coalition that pledged to fight the central administration's resistance to change.

As pressure mounted from a variety of media and civic organizations, Mayor Washington called together business representatives, parents, reformers, educators, and representatives of the board and the teachers union and had the second summit on education. On 11 October 1987, Washington and his staff expected no more than four hundred people to attend the open forum at the University of Illinois-Chicago campus. Despite modest expectations, more than one thousand parents, community organizers, students, teachers, and taxpayers attended. Due to the unexpected level of enthusiasm for and interest in school reform, the mayor established the Parent/Community Council as a special subcommittee to the summit.

The summit was charged by the mayor with making recommendations that could later be translated into legislation. The challenge would be to achieve consensus about the shape of reform among the various constituencies. But the importance of the summit lay less in its formal charge and more in the creation of a new form for interest group negotiations, a form that legitimizes the policy of interest representation. Without this new format, the traditional battle between the groups would not have justified the creation of a policy that involves parents as a legitimate interest. The summit became a deliberative forum in which representation was based on functional rather than popular principles (Anderson 1979).

Writing almost twenty years ago, Peterson (1976) placed his emphasis on understanding how the Chicago Board of Education made policy. He equated the decision making that goes on within the board with school politics. He was following the tradition of looking at political systems, assuming that the board made decisions based on the relative strengths of outside pressures. But Mayor Washington created a new ad hoc mechanism outside the board of education to allow other interests a seat at the policy-making table. Representatives of parent and advocacy groups were invited to the summit and played an important role in defining what the issues were. They became instant players.

Earlier efforts at decentralization in New York and Detroit were similarly shaped by forces beyond the traditional educational political system. The Ford Foundation played a central role in the New York effort by funding various community groups (LaNoue and Smith 1973). In Chicago, the summit had the effect of raising the legitimacy and visibility of outside reform organizations in the discussions of reform. Additionally, foundations augmented the advocacy and research activities of a few of the educational reform groups and later funded organizations to help with the implementation and study of the reform (McKersie 1993).

When the summit was convened, the nine-member board of education had a majority of minority members. One former member of the board of education felt that Mayor Washington had pulled together a surprisingly broad-based coalition, which fell apart after his sudden death in 1987, just a few months after the summit had started:

Clearly, at the point that the strike occurred, no one would have agreed to a memorandum of understanding that would have used the summit as a vehicle. The mayor asking the "heads of state" so to speak really had a way of saying to people, this is what is in everyone's best interest so sign on to it. And there were none of us who didn't think it was the right way to go. And his creation of the Parent/Community Council to the summit was very important. Up until that point there had been no voice of parents or community in the entire process. I think that when he passed away what we saw was a clear vacuum in leadership, where you saw people running every which way to do whatever they could however they could.

Others have also acknowledged this leadership vacuum after Washington's death (Hess 1991; McKersie 1993; O'Connell 1991). At the city politics level, the coalition that had supported Washington was divided when Eugene Sawyer, an African American alderman, was voted in as interim mayor. Supporters of Washington wanted Timothy Evans, another African American alderman, as mayor. Sawyer's ultimate election was supported primarily by white aldermen who had, in the past, opposed Washington.

In terms of school politics, Sawyer put Erwin France in charge of getting the summit recommendations into a coherent policy. France replaced Hal Baron, who had been appointed to that task by Mayor Washington. France was viewed as part of the traditional government establishment, with ties to the school reform movement (Hess 1991). In addition, once Sawyer took office, one respondent felt that the "major concern was to protect the Mayor from a 'bad' package," and so the mayor's office was unwilling to take a strong position on anything the summit produced.

It was months before the recommendations of the summit were published, and it took even longer for France to transform them into legislative language. But by then subgroups of the summit were pushing for different forms of the legislation in Springfield. To protect its own interests, the board of education did the same. One board member stated, "The board felt obligated, we felt we had a responsibility, to submit our own package as we felt it ought to be submitted." The business community drafted its own bill, as did a coalition of groups called CURE (Chicagoans United to Reform Education, headed up by Designs for Change) and the Parent/Community Council. By the end of March 1988, there were eight reform proposals out, including the one from the summit (Chicago Panel 1988).

Most of the reform groups were linked to some extent by their common interest in transforming the structure of the Chicago public school system. These groups provided the content for the reform packages. The business and civic reform groups provided access to increased private and foundation financial support. The community and social reform groups contributed their network of grassroots activists and volunteers. One example of the collective effort was the formation of ABCS (Alliance for Better Chicago Schools), an umbrella organization comprising many of the city's reform groups. It tried to coordinate the lobbying and legislative drafting efforts in Springfield. Other coalitions (such as CURE) and organizations (such as the Chicago Panel) were subsumed under ABCS for the purposes of passing the reform bill. The efforts of these various groups were quite fluid.

An important element of decentralization in Chicago was the focus on legislative change. The reform groups' collective goal was some form of legislative change that would restructure the Chicago school system, ultimately Senate Bill 1839 (later signed into law as S.B. 1840). Hess (1991) justifies why the reform organizations took a legislative approach, stating that there was no "willingness" on the part of the board and superintendent to "power share" without some outside stimulus to force the issue.

This was principally thought to be the fault of Superintendent Manford Byrd, Jr. Byrd had worked himself up through the Chicago public school system, starting as a teacher in 1954 and becoming deputy superintendent in 1968 (McClory 1987). He had been passed over as superintendent a number of times before being appointed to that position in 1984. Hess wrote of Byrd:

> [T]he general superintendent was focused on power accumulation, rather than power sharing. His budget proposals progressively drained resources from the schools while expanding the bureaucratic empire. He accused those who questioned his priorities of "trashing" the public schools and, referring to their support by foundations, of "pimping off the miseries of low income students." (p. 120)

Byrd, in discussing the reform after its initial passage in July 1988, expressed his belief that the reform was only about power:

> [T]he reform package is more about power than education. They make the assumption that we can share the power and that from that redefinition of power and the relocation of the centers of power, achievement will flow.

The superintendent's feeling was that reform needed to be about motivating students by creating tangible incentives, training teachers, and having strong principals who lead, rather than about shifting power. Byrd was asked to resign in 1989.

Obviously, community organizations gained tremendous credibility in the face of the superintendent's intransigence. To force change in the system, organizations took their requests to the state legislature. In the General Assembly, the school reform bill was influenced along partisan and geographic dimensions. Many Republicans sought to dissolve the board's overall jurisdiction over the Chicago public school system's $2 billion budget, 450,000 students, and almost 600 schools. Many Republicans joined State Senator Bob Kustra in an attempt to create twenty separate school districts and boards. However, Democrats controlled the Illinois General Assembly. A bill originally sponsored by State Senator Arthur Berman sought to maintain the board's overall jurisdiction but increase the authority and discretion of existing local school improvement councils. Even though Berman initially sponsored the legislation, House Speaker Michael Madigan controlled enough House votes to effectively determine legislative outcomes.

As the speaker for the Democratic majority, Madigan was a very influential politician in Illinois. Although he represented an ethnic South Side district in Chicago, Madigan and many of his constituents were products and consumers of Chicago's parochial school system and had little interest in the public schools. Many believed that Madigan's interest in shaping educational reform in Chicago was political rather than substantive. One Republican senator criticized Madigan's motives:

> Madigan couldn't leave Springfield without a school reform bill because he was publicly and privately being tagged with killing the tax increase. Politically, I think he wanted to leave Springfield with a school reform bill. Ironically, I think Madigan, and most legislators would agree, doesn't give two hoots about the Chicago Public Schools. He sent his kids to parochial schools; his district is dominated with parochial schools.

Having defeated the governor's tax increase, Madigan needed a more positive victory to demonstrate to the people of Chicago that he shared their concerns. Once he had set the ground rule that the reform had to be revenue-neutral, he took aggressive measures to insure its passage. The reformers accepted his ground rules.

The school reform bill (at this point, S.B. 1839) had been approved by just one vote in the senate when it went to the house for

approval. Madigan organized a caucus that met in his office in Springfield to hash out the specific language of the law with the help of his
aides. According to one of his aides, the process was "democratic" and
the shape of the law was determined by a broad-based coalition of
groups: "In eight years—this was the first time I saw 75 to 80 people
in one room hammering out, line by line, a major piece of legislation."
However, other observers identified two groups that were overrepresented in Madigan's caucus. Reform groups, particularly Don Moore
of Designs for Change, and representatives of Chicago business, particularly Warren Bacon of Chicago United (the community groups representing business interests), were cited as the most influential players
by those who participated in the reform process. Several observers
concurred with the observations of one of our respondents, a lawyer
and lobbyist for the board of education: "[Madigan's] education staff
person, as well as other people acting on his behalf...clearly were
allowing CURE [the Designs for Change coalition] and Chicago United to write the bill."

In particular, the traditional power structure was left out of the
process. Representatives of the Chicago Board of Education recognized that they were intentionally excluded from the legislative
process. Another respondent, a lobbyist for the board, described how
board representatives were not invited to the first meetings. Later,
when the board offered input in the rewriting of the bill, "[We] were
accused of trying to change the meaning of certain passages and we
said we were just trying to make it workable." The bill passed the
house on 2 July 1988. After some revisions it was rewritten as Senate
Bill 1840 and signed into law on 12 December 1988.

THE ISSUE OF RACE

Madigan desired, but ultimately did not need, black Democratic support for the school reform bill. The Black Democratic Caucus, led by
State Senator Richard Newhouse and dominated by Chicago legislators, resisted Madigan's legislative control over an issue that deeply
affected and impacted black constituents in Chicago.

The issue of racial politics was raised by the Black Caucus and by
black members of the board of education, including Superintendent

Byrd. In an interview soon after the bill was first passed in July 1988, one respondent from the Chicago Panel, stated, "The Superintendent [Byrd] cast the reform effort as a racist strategy by two 'white boys' [Don Moore, of Designs for Change, and G. Alfred Hess, of the Chicago Panel]. But...the genesis of reform was from a black mayor [Washington] concerned about potential political problems." Another respondent, a member of the board of education when the bill was first passed and part of Operation Push (a black community organization started by Jesse Jackson), publicly stated her opposition to the bill. And, in speaking with us, she said, "I see this as a move probably to take the city of Chicago out of black control. It's kind of strange that until we had a majority of blacks on the board and a majority of women, there's a cry for reform."

In his account of both the passage and the initial implementation of the Chicago school reform bill, Hess (1991) raises the issue of racial politics and downplays its importance. After the bill was signed into law, Hess writes about how race entered the picture during the interim mayoral elections of January 1989. State's Attorney Richard M. Daley (son of former mayor Richard J. Daley) entered the election and chose school reform as the "cornerstone of his campaign for mayor" (Hess 1991, p. 168). Blacks who were currently part of the power structure were thus immediately suspect of the reform, and, once Daley was elected mayor, opposed any action he took on the reform.

The motives of the reformers are not suspect here. What we find, from even the simplest accounts of the reform process, is how a traditional power structure—the state legislature, led by whites—ultimately controlled both the passage of the reform and its implementation. One observer during the legislative process privately noted that legislators were trying to decide whether to vote for the bill based on what would be most damaging to (then) Mayor Eugene Sawyer.

O'Connell (1991) addressed the question of why traditional black organizations were not involved with or supportive of the reform. Some of the community leaders she spoke with suggested that the organizations were caught up in the political fight for the mayor's office. Others believed that some of the black leadership recognized that they were not going to defeat the white businesses, or that the black leadership thought that asking "poor blacks and others to turn their schools around" was asking too much (p. 34).

There is evidence of black grassroots support for the reform, but black middle-class leadership was conflicted about how to relate to the new reform organizations that were springing up. With both the board and the teachers union on the defensive, the black middle class and its representatives were unable to mount a serious alternative to the reform initiatives.

CONTROLLING INTERESTS

Respondents with whom we spoke named three groups as influential in shaping the bill that ultimately became law. Business (particularly Chicago United), reform groups (particularly Designs for Change), and legislators (particularly Michael Madigan) were most frequently cited as influential. Local parents were rarely mentioned; and typical interests, such as the CTU and the board of education, exerted little or no influence. This result is extraordinary for those versed in the assumptions of interest-group liberalism, for it suggests that the very interests that one would have expected to have voice in deliberations were without much say. Qualities other than those that pluralists would identify as important (i.e., jobs, legal authority) were determining who was sitting at the table and influencing the direction of the legislation. The teachers strike and the failure of the board and the CTU to make a persuasive case for their approach to the problems delegitimized their participation, creating an opportunity for new voices—in this case, those who represented the parent and community interests that Washington had brought to the table. The way those interests were defined depended a great deal on professional reformers.

Despite the portrayal of the reform as a movement from the parents, in some cases parents could not gain representation in the process. One parent who was part of the Parent/Community Council met with members of her community to create the Black Coalition for Education Reform. They set up community forums to discuss reform and hired a lobbyist, yet were unable to gain recognition from the legislature. No members of this group were represented as part of the special task force in Madigan's office. In this parent's view, "[T]he legislation was forced through by power and money."

In contrast, a staff person for Chicago United listed how the business community marshaled resources to help the bill pass: hiring lawyers to draft the legislation pertaining to oversight authority, sending advocates on corporate jets to Springfield to meet with the governor and state legislators, hiring a lobbying firm to lobby for the bill. Chicago United believed their involvement could be "a model for corporate involvement for other cities."

Whether the legislative process was exclusive or inclusive, respondents agree that Madigan set one very firm ground rule before negotiations could begin: there would be no new funding for the Chicago public school system. All proposals for reform were subject to discussion and negotiation unless they involved the implementation of new programs or the hiring of new staff. For two reasons, this ground rule proved key in enabling the reformers to set the agenda. First, the empowerment ideology focuses not on the necessity for additional financing, but on the inadequacies of bureaucratic performance and the essential role of power in its diagnosis of the problems. Second, the board and the CTU, far more than did reform groups, always headed their list of requirements for school reform with the insistence that more funding was needed; such a view was in high disfavor in Madigan's Springfield and ultimately would not prevail.

In our analysis, the rules set by the state legislature controlled the representation of interests. We use Schmitter's (1979) definition of the term *corporatism* to describe interest groups' controlled role in the policy-making arena. *Corporatism* refers to the way the organizations are "granted a deliberate representational monopoly within their respective categories in exchange for observing certain controls on their selection of leaders and articulation of demands and supports" (p. 16). In the case of Chicago school reform, particular organizations were given a representational monopoly in writing the reform bill, and this was done, in part, because these reform groups were willing to have their desire for increased revenue "controlled" by the state legislature.

The no-funding parameter effectively empowered the state legislators to decide who had a voice in the reform, and what kind of voice that would be. In a retreat sponsored by various foundations just before the final version of the bill was passed,[2] reformers discussed "phase II" of Chicago school reform, contemplating what they should do to get the state legislature to allocate additional monies to the schools. One member at the retreat said of the legislature, "We called their bluff in June, they said there is no money, so we got a revenue-neutral bill. We have to show real change and some numbers in the spring so that we may get new resources." Other retreat participants stated that they needed to "start talking with legislators who already pledged their support for more money." It seems that rather than ask for the additional monies they knew the schools needed, reformers instead backed a revenue-neutral bill for the sake of change. Yet without additional resources, the reformers and the school system were now in the position of proving that the system could change even without revenue. It seems a two-edged sword: If they can change without revenue, why provide it?

One parent who took part in the summit and was a cochair of the Parent/Community Council was disappointed in how the reform turned out. He said that during the reform negotiations there "were two kinds of groups...one group was saying 'reform first, money later'...the other group was saying 'money, everything.' The 'reform first, money later' faction won out. It is a shame. It is a real shame this happened." This parent characterized the reform groups that backed the bill as "misguided."

Some of the people we spoke with argued that the lack of new funds as a provision of the legislation meant that middle-class schools would improve while the schools that were located in poorer areas, with fewer resources, would get worse. One former member of the board expressed this point of view:

> Poor parents lose. They will need to purchase more technical assistance than other parents and gaps will become wider between rich and poor schools. It will become a two-tier system.

In fact, half of all Chicago public schools have no support from outside resources, whereas others have access to a variety of support and resources (McKersie 1993).

The no-new-revenue rule also controlled what issues were taken on by various interest groups. For instance, the CTU, recognizing that there would be no additional monies for the schools, lobbied to protect their contract. According to Jacqueline Vaughn, president of the

CTU, the issue of teacher remediation was key. Certain parties in the Madigan caucus wanted to give principals greater authority to fire incompetent teachers. But the teachers union fought to limit that authority, and won. In a CTU newsletter just after the bill was passed, Vaughn said, "There were a number of business, political and so-called education leaders who were intent on using education reform as a vehicle for destroying the Chicago Teachers Union and turning the clock back decades in terms of employees' rights and working conditions" (Chicago Teachers Union 1988).

The degree of authority and accountability for school principals was vigorously debated in Springfield while the legislation was being negotiated. Reform groups, including Designs for Change and the Parent/Community Council, pushed for local school councils that would be dominated by parents and have the authority to hire and fire principals. A representative of Designs for Change explained why he thought this was an important element of school reform:

> It removes the political exchange system. Before, school staff were only accountable to those who were above them, people who weren't interested in improving things. This bill changes that. The principal now has real accountability to the major consumer groups—the parents, staff, and community.

According to one representative of the business community, the Chicago Principals Association felt this provision of the bill gave principals too much accountability and not enough authority to manage their school. Unions besides CTU, which represented the other staff in the schools, resisted an increase in principals' authority. Eventually, principals won the right to give directions to all their staff, including engineers and cafeteria workers. In addition, principals won the right to hire teachers for vacant positions by ability rather than seniority.

A more difficult issue to resolve was the principals' obligation to accept "supernumeraries." Supernumeraries are the two hundred to three hundred teachers who lose their posts each year because of declining enrollment at their schools. Such teachers had the right, according to CTU contract, to choose the school to which they would move, and the principal had no alternative but to accept such teachers.

The legislation that emerged from negotiations in Springfield required supernumeraries to apply for new positions. After three rejections by the principals of the schools to which they apply, the teachers would be assigned to vacancies for a period of one year. Principals must follow seniority, however, in deciding which teachers must go when enrollment declines (Lenz 1989).

Chicago's business community, particularly Chicago United, fought for some kind of oversight provision that would force the Chicago Board of Education to implement reform. Warren Bacon, of Chicago United, wanted to make sure that the board was not obstructionist in the implementation of the new law and advocated an oversight committee with the power to fire members of the board if they were uncooperative. One respondent, a lawyer for Chicago United and a former board member, lobbied in Springfield for this provision: "Even if I were on the board, I would support it, there's too many things you have to worry about as a board member to be able to handle all the aspects of implementing something like this reform."

Opposition to such an oversight committee came from various quarters. Naturally, members of the board opposed it. One member of the interim board expressed the opinion that the oversight provision represented the interests of a predominantly white state legislature attempting to control a minority system:

> I think the oversight authority is just an attempt to control the Chicago public school system by the state legislature. It's interesting that with this whole issue of control, they will not accept the responsibility, nor will they be held accountable for providing the resources, in this case the dollars, which they are legally responsible to provide to the Chicago public schools. I think it's a power grab by the state legislature to control a minority school system and make it beholden to someone else.

Other board members also felt it removed all power from the board. As one board member said, "It makes us a toothless tiger." Even some business representatives reported their opposition to an oversight committee on the grounds that it would add another layer of bureaucracy. A representative of the Chicago Chamber of Commerce said,

"In a day where there is a cry for 'chop at the top' and a bloated bureaucracy, they have created two bureaucracies, the oversight, and the mini [local] boards."

According to several observers, Harold Washington's successor as mayor of Chicago, Eugene Sawyer, wanted to insure that the governor did not control any oversight committee that might emerge from these negotiations. Apparently, Republican legislators wanted Illinois's Republican governor to have at least equal, if not primary, authority over the composition of the oversight committee. Mayor Sawyer's aide Erwin France lobbied intensively for a provision to have the mayor appoint the majority of those committee members. According to a member of the Chicago Panel, France gained the support of black legislators who would not agree to support the legislation unless Sawyer controlled the oversight authority. Republicans would not support it under those conditions. One respondent reported, "[S]o the Speaker [Madigan] had to decide whether to give control of the oversight committee to the Mayor to keep the Black Caucus in line or to split the authority to get the Republicans on board. The Chicago Panel wanted a split authority. This was in the bill on June 30 when the bill fell short by one vote."

Mayor Sawyer won control of the oversight committee in the final legislation. However, in the second incarnation of the bill, the oversight provision was dropped and the powers of the School Finance Authority were expanded.

THE CONTENTS OF REFORM LEGISLATION

The key provisions of the school reform bill are these:

1. Every school would have a local school council (LSC) with eleven members: six parents, two teachers, two community residents, and the principal. The council will be able to select the school principal and decide whether or not to renew the principal's four-year performance contract. The LSC, and other members of the school community, will develop a three-year School Improvement Plan. It will also have the right to approve or disapprove the entire school budget. In addition, a professional personnel advisory com-

mittee composed of teachers will advise the principal and LSC on educational matters.

2. District councils will be composed of one LSC member from each district school. These twenty-three councils will be able to select their district superintendent and decide whether or not to renew his or her four-year performance contract. Each district council will elect a member to serve on the Board Nominating Commission, along with five individuals selected by the mayor. This commission will select three school board candidates for each board opening to present to the mayor for appointment.

3. Principals will be able to select educational staff for all new and vacant positions, based on merit and ability. They will also be able to release teachers who receive an unsatisfactory rating after a forty-five-day in-school remediation period.

4. State Chapter 1 funds are appropriated each year to the Chicago Public Schools to fund programs for low-income students. In the past, the board has used those funds for general programs. In the reform, 100 percent of Chapter 1 monies must be used for supplementary programs such as early childhood education, tutoring, and lowering of class size. The loss in revenue to the board's budget will be made up by a ceiling that will be put on administrative spending.

5. In the final version of the bill, the separate oversight committee was replaced with expanded powers for the preexisting School Finance Authority. The authority would monitor the implementation of this legislation and make annual reports to the public, the mayor, the governor and the leadership of the General Assembly. It was also provided that these new powers would terminate in June 1994.

6. No new revenue.

Although the majority of respondents support the new legislation as a step in the right direction, they debate three aspects of the bill— the value of local management of the schools, the reform of governance over "educational" reform, and the lack of revenue attached to the legislation. And, as we have tried to argue, those three aspects encompassed democracy, an attack on institutions, and the maintenance of status quo resources, and that is what made the bill palatable to the basically white, suburban, and rural interests that held the balance of power in passing the reform.

CONCLUSION

Ultimately, Chicago school reform factors a new interest into the formal authority structure of the Chicago public school system—parents and community members. In some ways it also limits the outside voice of key pressure groups, such as Designs for Change. Such groups have for a long time been attempting to change the way a government bureaucracy does business. Now their interests have been made a part of that bureaucracy, and their members have legal responsibilities for the operation of that system. The state is transformed by the absorption of this interest at the same time as the interest is transformed by becoming part of the state. Because parents and community representatives hold majority positions on the LSCs and have a large say in both who is on the school board and who is the principal, they must assume responsibility for how the system performs and thus lose some credibility as nonpartisan outsiders. Parents either cease to be considered a unified interest, if LSC members differ with other parents in the school on particular issues, or the interests of the parents become associated with the administration of the schools and the system in general. The state gains legitimacy by co-opting the outside interest. Although some parents and community members might gain authority in their new roles, they can no longer maintain their authoritative position as outsiders.

Furthermore, reform in Chicago must be understood in the context of the transformation of urban politics and the state. The success of the reform depended on Mayor Washington's incorporating outside interests into decision making about reform and putting his "moral weight" behind those interests in the deliberation. It also depended upon the people who represented those interests in the deliberations. They proved skilled in the negotiations, arguing forcefully for their analysis of what the problems were in Chicago. The representatives of the key institutional actors were ill prepared for the battles that followed and had lost much of their credibility with legislators who needed to show some action without fundamentally violating the racial status quo. Finally, school reform depended on meeting the requirements of the state legislature. The development of LSCs was an idea that survived the Illinois state legislature because reform groups offered a plan that asked for no new revenue. Reform was defined to mean the incorporation of the parent interest in the process of bureaucratic decision making. This result was congruent with the ideology of the reformers and the interests of the politicians, particularly those who felt little sympathy for the teachers or the board.

The politics of inclusion, as they have played out in Chicago, disperse both the power of parents and the overall capacity of the system to articulate its own interests beyond the call for more attention to parent and community interests in school policy making. Wider questions of learning and poverty devolved to the local school, where they are negotiated at the school building level. Those schools with the fewest resources and whose students begin school with the most problems are least likely to see the advantages of this effort to reorganize schooling. Those schools with substantial financial and other resources to draw upon will likely do well in this environment. While changes in governance structure made sense to reformers, they also made sense to politicians driven by a different kind of thinking. The results placed a huge amount of pressure on a very weakly developed constituency that was not in a position to overcome many powerful forces operating in the policy environment, especially as the locus of that conflict moved beyond the school building.

NOTES

Sue Reed and Michael Heise assisted in the early analysis and writing of this chapter.

1. Most of the quotations in this chapter were drawn from forty-three interviews conducted in July and August 1988, just after the school reform bill (Senate Bill 1839) was passed by the state legislature for the first time. These interviews were open-ended, and we asked respondents to reflect on who the major players were, who had won or lost, and what they thought of the bill. See the Appendix for a description of this sample.

2. The retreat was held on 9 and 10 December 1988. One of the authors (Nakagawa) attended the retreat as a participant-observer.

Chapter 6

Representative Democracy: Comparing and Contrasting the Attitudes of Chicago Parents

Chapter 5 detailed much of the essential history of the Chicago school reform. While the evolution of P.A. 85-1418 may be traceable through its variations and influences, the attitudes that gave birth to it are more fleeting and elusive. Where did such historic legislation spring from? There is a common perception, essentially true, that the American population at large has grown weary of academic mediocrity. But even given the truth in such a belief, how does that perception hold up when applied to those much-discussed clients of the school system, the urban school parents? If the Chicago school reform was a revolution in bureaucracy and decentralization, is it accurate to portray Chicago parents as angered and storming the gates of the school board? In this chapter we examine the common assumptions in regard to urban school parents, and find that these perceptions, by and large, do not hold up.

The implicit building block of many current school reforms is representative democracy. Empowerment policies of decentralization assume that greater democracy—manifested by increased involvement of parents and community members—will naturally improve the educational system. Chicago's LSCs are representative democracy in action, with six parents representing the interests of all parents at a particular school.

An assumption of representative democracy, and an assumption implicit in the political design of Chicago school reform policy, is that people who are elected to governance positions represent those who elect them, that the parent representatives will reflect the interests of parents in the policies they make. In the case of the LSCs, the parents who are elected are assumed to have a set of interests different from those of the administrators who were running the system prior to the reform. Although there might be differences between parents as to what policies ought to be pursued, the parents will have more in common with each other than they will with other interest groups, leading to the parent majority's making policies together. If these assumptions are not true, then serious questions emerge about how different the new elites will be from the elites they replaced.

In pushing an empowerment model of reform, reformers believed that parents were dissatisfied and saw many problems in the system. Using a telephone survey of 378 Chicago parents, we compare the attitudes and perceptions of Chicago public school parents with those of Chicago private school parents to discover the extent of public school dissatisfaction. In addition, using interviews with 50 parents serving on an LSC, we look at whether LSC parent attitudes differ from the public school parents they purport to represent.

Our findings suggest that the majority of parents, regardless of racial background, socioeconomic status, or serving on the LSC, tend to support what takes place in their own schools. Parent attitudes are generally positive about their children's schooling, leading one to conclude that parents are fairly content with the educational system in Chicago. Satisfaction levels were surprisingly high, especially in areas that have direct effect on the child: teaching quality, how the teacher treats the child, and how much the teacher helps the child. And although it might be expected that drugs, low achievement, school cleanliness, child safety, and other such issues would be identified most often as problems in the schools, this was not the case. Generally such issues were identified as problems by fewer than half of the parents, and the issue identified as a problem more than any other was lack of parental involvement in the schools.

Such opinions might be unexpected given the general perception of the Chicago public schools, but they are not unprecedented. Wasley (1993), in a research project to study school change, asks the question, "What is it that parents want from their schools, and what role might parents play in both determining and achieving those ends?" What she and her colleagues found was that basically parents wanted information: about how the school was changing, about how to talk to school personnel if the need arose, about whether the school was "challenging" their children (pp. 723–24). Relatedly, the roles parents wanted to play in the school had to do with opportunities: to think with educators about the schools, to get other parents involved, to have their opinions heard. With respect to the Chicago school reform, Wasley states, "I am not convinced that absolute power equalization such as Chicago has developed is what parents want or need to be influential in changing schools. Nor am I convinced that it is sufficient" (p. 726). The opinions stated by the parents in our survey seem to verify Wasley's conclusion.

It is possible that these high levels of satisfaction and low perceptions of problems are *a result of* the first year of Chicago school reform. Because we have no measures of parent perceptions prior to the first year of reform, it is difficult to ascertain what changes took place in parents as a result of the reform. But it is unlikely that changes that took place in the schools were so drastic as to cause parents to become satisfied in one year. And it is very possible that parents were satisfied with their schools to begin with. In *A Place Called School* (1984), Goodlad also questions the idea that parents are as dissatisfied with their schools as the popular press would have us believe:

> It is one thing to be critical of schooling, especially when one reads or hears regularly that the schools are doing a poor job. It is quite another to think similarly about "my child's school." (pp. 33–34)

Goodlad found his reasoning to be correct. In his survey of parents throughout the country, just 10 percent of parents gave their own schools a grade of a D or F. Instead, most parents rated their schools a B.

Similarly, our results show that parents in Chicago are much more critical of the public school system as a whole than they are of their own child's school. When we asked parents to grade the Chicago public school system, 14 percent of public school parents and 28 percent of local school council parents gave the Chicago public school system as a whole a grade of a D or F. But when questioned about how satisfied they were with their own child's school, over 80 percent of parents were very or somewhat satisfied.

Although LSC parents tended to be a bit more critical than other public school parents, the fact that LSC parents were not significantly different in their attitudes from the public school parents in the phone survey leads us to conclude that Chicago parents are, in general, satisfied with what is occurring in their individual schools. The perceptions of reformers during the reform movement were that "parents were desperate" and "people were mad as hell" (O'Connell 1991, p. 8). The results of this chapter demonstrate that parents are likely to get involved for reasons other than their dissatisfaction with the schools. Perhaps parents who are satisfied with their schools are more likely to get involved in and support what is already taking place in the school. Or perhaps parents would rather supplement school professionals in the existing school policies rather than reform the school and tell school professionals what to do.

From these findings we conclude that parents' attitudes and perceptions support an enablement model of school reform rather than an empowerment one. With the empowerment model we would have expected to find that parents were not satisfied with their schools, that they identified many school problems, and that they were more active in policy-type activities than in supportive activities. Instead, parents expressed fairly high levels of satisfaction, identified few problems, and participated more frequently in supportive than in policy activities.

With respect to the different samples, private school parents were more satisfied and perceived fewer problems in their schools than did public school parents. But we found few differences between the public school parents and the LSC parents, suggesting that LSC parents reflect other parents' attitudes and that these LSC parents hold attitudes more in line with an enablement model than with an empowerment model.

These findings do not totally discount the empowerment model. Neither do they completely support the enablement model. Instead, they should be interpreted as a way of modifying both the enablement and the empowerment models to better complement parents' own motivations. Because this survey did not explicitly set out to test these models, the measures of satisfaction, problem identification, attitudes toward parent involvement, and reported frequency of involvement are just indicators of the underlying parent motivations, not definitive answers to why parents get involved.

In the following reports of frequencies, the phrase *public school parents* refers only to the 253 public school parents from the phone survey, and *LSC parents* refers only to the random sample of 50 parents who served on an LSC. For a complete description of the methodology and sample, see the Appendix.

FINDINGS

Levels of Satisfaction

Overall school satisfaction. Table 6.1 contains information about satisfaction levels of private school parents, public school parents, and LSC parents. The 378 parents we polled in the telephone survey and the 50 LSC parents tended to be satisfied with their schools. We asked parents to rate how satisfied they were with various aspects of their schools, either "very satisfied," "somewhat satisfied," "somewhat dissatisfied," or "very dissatisfied." Over 80 percent of all parents were somewhat or very satisfied with their child's school in general. Private school parents were more satisfied with their schools than were public school parents; 96 percent of private school parents were very satisfied or somewhat satisfied with the child's school overall, whereas just over 86 percent of public school parents were somewhat or very satisfied with their schools overall. The 50 LSC parents expressed satisfaction levels equal to those of public school parents: 86 percent of the LSC parents were somewhat or very satisfied with the quality of their child's school overall.

Point totals were given to each answer in order to calculate mean satisfaction levels for each group. These mean scores are reported in Table 6.1. Very satisfied equaled 3.0, somewhat satisfied 2.0, somewhat dissatisfied 1.0, and very dissatisfied 0.0. A one-way analysis of variance on the private school and public school samples found that the difference between public and private school mean satisfaction scores for the overall school was significant ($F[1, 374] = 22.5, p < .0001$). But

Table 6.1
Percentages of Parents Somewhat or Very Satisfied and Mean Satisfaction Scores,
by Private School, Public School, and LSC Parents

	Private[a]	*Public*[b]	*LSC*[c]
Overall school satisfaction	96%	86%	86%
	2.64	2.26	2.16
	(0.64)	(0.77)	(0.71)
Quality of teaching	97%	85%	84%
	2.67	2.27	2.14
	(0.59)	(0.81)	(0.71)
How teacher treats child	94%	87%	88%
	2.66	2.44	2.34
	(0.63)	(0.80)	(0.69)
Teacher help	93%	82%	84%
	2.60	2.33	2.26
	(0.70)	(0.89)	(0.78)
Time spent on reading and math	87%	77%	68%
	2.59	2.33	2.21
	(0.73)	(0.84)	(0.97)
Discipline	94%	76%	68%
	2.72	2.21	2.02
	(0.56)	(0.99)	(0.96)
Information the school provides	89%	79%	78%
	2.55	2.22	2.16
	(0.76)	(0.97)	(0.96)
Class size	89%	68%	64%
	2.48	2.00	1.72
	(0.74)	(0.98)	(1.00)
Afterschool activities	71%	57%	48%
	2.27	2.04	1.59
	(0.88)	(0.99)	(1.06)
School grounds	97%	82%	68%
	2.74	2.14	1.96
	(0.49)	(0.92)	(1.00)
School reform	—	67%	90%
	—	2.34	2.34
	—	(1.86)	(0.71)

Note. Standard deviations are in parentheses.

[a] *n* = 125.
[b] *n* = 253.
[c] *n* = 50.

Table 6.2

Percentages of Parents Somewhat or Very Satisfied with School Qualities,
Public School and LSC Parents, by Race

	General Public[a]			LSC[b]		
	Black (%)	White (%)	Hispanic (%)	Black (%)	White (%)	Hispanic (%)
Overall	89	81	86	83	88	89
Quality of teaching	86	84	87	75	87	100
How teacher treats child	89	85	87	88	88	89
Teacher help	82	80	85	88	81	78
Time spent on reading and math	81	75	74	62	63	89
Discipline	75	75	76	62	69	78
Information the school provides	78	78	81	71	81	89
Class size	72	63	62	75	56	44
Afterschool activities	59	54	58	42	50	56
School grounds	34	22	32	25	6	22
School reform	74	66	66	95	88	89

[a] Black $n = 122$, white $n = 68$, Hispanic $n = 53$.
[b] Black $n = 24$, white $n = 16$, Hispanic $n = 9$.

the difference between the public school and the LSC parent mean satisfaction scores was not significant.

Table 6.2 reports the satisfaction of public school parents and LSC parents by race. On the question of satisfaction with the school overall, again over 80 percent of black, white, and Hispanic parents from both the general public school parent sample and the LSC sample were somewhat or very satisfied. The black public school parents were more satisfied than the black LSC parents—89 percent of black public school parents were satisfied with their child's school, whereas 83 percent of black LSC parents responded similarly. Within the public school parent sample, white parents had lower levels of satisfaction than did black or Hispanic parents, and black parents had the highest levels of satisfaction. In contrast, for the LSC sample, the black parents had the lowest levels of satisfaction, with white parents and Hispanic parents having nearly identical levels of satisfaction.

Satisfaction with teaching. The high degrees of satisfaction with the school overall were echoed in questions about satisfaction with aspects of teaching. Table 6.1 shows that over 80 percent of all parents were somewhat or very satisfied with the quality of teaching at their school, whether from a public or a private school, or whether an LSC member or not. Over 80 percent of all parents were also somewhat or very satisfied with the help teachers give their child, and with how teachers treat their child. Private school parents were the most satisfied with all aspects of teaching at their child's school, with LSC and other public school parents having lower but similar levels of satisfaction.

The mean satisfaction scores for all aspects of teaching reflected this. Scores from private school parents were significantly higher than those from public school parents (all at the $p < .01$ level). However, as with satisfaction with the school overall, there were no statistically significant differences in the average satisfaction scores for public and LSC parents, although LSC parents had lower average scores than did other parents.

In Table 6.2 we see that public school parents did not significantly differ by race in the levels of satisfaction with aspects of teaching at their child's school. Over 80 percent of black, white, and Hispanic public school parents were somewhat or very satisfied with the quality of teaching, the help teachers give, and the way teachers treat their child. Among black parents, public school parents had higher levels of satisfaction with the quality of teaching (86 percent answered somewhat or very satisfied) than did LSC parents (75 percent). However, white and Hispanic LSC parents had higher levels of satisfaction with the quality of teaching than did white and Hispanic public school parents in general. Similarly, in terms of how parents feel their child is treated by the teachers at their school, black LSC parents again had lower levels of satisfaction than did black public school parents, with white and Hispanic LSC parents having higher levels of satisfaction than white and Hispanic public school parents.

In contrast, on the question of the help teachers give their child, black LSC parents had higher levels of satisfaction than did black public school parents. Of black LSC parents, 88 percent were somewhat or very satisfied, in comparison to 82 percent of black public school parents in general. White LSC parents also had slightly higher levels of satisfaction than did white public school parents (81 percent and 80 percent, respectively). The Hispanic LSC parents had lower levels of satisfaction than did the Hispanic public school parents from the phone survey—78 percent of Hispanic LSC parents were somewhat or very satisfied with the help teachers give, in comparison to 85 percent of Hispanic public school parents in general.

Satisfaction with school policies. Three questions focused on parents' satisfaction with school policies—amount of time spent on reading and math, amount of discipline, and amount of information the school provides about how the child is doing. From Table 6.1 we find that public school parents were less satisfied with the amount of time spent on reading and math than were private school parents, and LSC parents had lower levels of satisfaction than either group. Among private school parents, 87 percent ($M = 2.59$, $SD = .73$) were somewhat or very satisfied with the amount of time spent on reading and math at their school, in comparison to 77 percent ($M = 2.33$, $SD = .84$) of public school parents and just 68 percent of LSC parents ($M = 2.21$, $SD = .97$). Again, the difference between the private school parents and the public school parents was significant ($F[1, 374] = 8.34$, $p < .01$), but the disparity between the public school parents and the LSC parents was not.

Satisfaction with the amount of discipline in the schools was similar. Private school parents had the highest average satisfaction levels, followed by public school parents and LSC parents, with the contrast between private and public again being significant, but the difference between public and LSC not. Of private school parents, 94 percent said they were somewhat or very satisfied with the amount of discipline in their schools. Just over 75 percent of public school parents were somewhat or very satisfied with the amount of discipline, and LSC parents had the lowest levels of satisfaction, with 68 percent being somewhat or very satisfied. Satisfaction with amount of information provided on how the child is doing in school was no different: 89 percent of private school parents, in comparison to 79 percent of public school and 78 percent of LSC parents, were somewhat or very satisfied with the amount of information.

Table 6.2 shows that black public school parents had the highest levels of satisfaction with amount of time spent on reading and math (81 percent), while black LSC parents had the lowest levels of satisfaction (62 percent). White LSC parents were also less satisfied than were white public school parents in general, whereas Hispanic LSC parents were more satisfied with reading and math time than were Hispanic public school parents in general. With respect to amount of discipline, black and white LSC parents were again less satisfied than their public school counterparts and Hispanic LSC parents were again more satisfied than were other Hispanic public school parents. And on the question of the amount of information provided by the school, black LSC parents were less satisfied than were other black public school parents, whereas white and Hispanic LSC parents were more satisfied with this aspect of school policy than were white and Hispanic public school parents in general.

Class size and afterschool activities. In terms of class size, again public school and LSC parents were less satisfied than were private school parents. The same was true for afterschool activities, with LSC parents having the lowest levels of satisfaction on both questions. The question on afterschool activities was the only question for which the difference in mean scores for LSC parents and public school parents was significant ($F[1, 231] = 10.92$, $p < .01$), with the difference in scores for the public and private school parents being just barely significant ($F[1, 293] = 3.96, p < .05$).

Among public school parents alone, Hispanic parents were least satisfied with the size of their child's classes, and black parents were most satisfied. This was also true of the LSC sample, with black LSC parents being the most satisfied and Hispanic LSC parents the least.

With respect to afterschool activities, parents in all racial groups, regardless of being an LSC member of not, had low levels of satisfaction. Black LSC parents were the least satisfied, and black public school parents were the most satisfied. Whereas 42 percent of black LSC parents were somewhat or very satisfied with their school's afterschool activities, 59 percent of black public school parents from the phone survey were satisfied. Public school parents of all racial groups were a bit more satisfied with the afterschool activities than were LSC parents.

Satisfaction with school and grounds appearance. We asked one question about satisfaction with the school building and grounds—"How satisfied are you with the way the school and grounds look?" As shown in Table 6.1, LSC parents were the least satisfied with this aspect of their schools, with 68 percent somewhat or very satisfied with the school and grounds appearance. In contrast, over 80 percent of other public school parents were satisfied with the school and grounds appearance. Private school parents were extremely satisfied—over 95 percent of private school parents reported being satisfied with school and grounds appearance.

Within the public school sample alone, black parents were the most satisfied with the physical aspects of their school, with white parents being the least satisfied. Among the LSC parents, black LSC parents were the most satisfied with respect to school appearance. In general, all racial groups of LSC parents were more critical and less satisfied with the physical upkeep of their schools than were other public school parents.

School reform satisfaction. We asked public school and LSC parents, "How satisfied are you with how school reform is working in your school?" Public school parents were much less satisfied with how school reform was working, with just 67 percent being somewhat or very satisfied. In contrast, 90 percent of the LSC parents were somewhat or very satisfied with school reform. Although these frequency differences appear large, the average satisfaction scores for school reform were equal. In the racial breakdown in Table 6.2, black parents, whether part of the LSC or not, were more satisfied with how school reform was working than were white or Hispanic parents.

Problems in the Schools

Satisfaction levels are one measure of parent attitudes toward their children's education. Identification of school problems is another. We listed a number of issues for parents and asked whether the issue was a big problem, some problem, or almost no problem in their child's school. Tables 6.3 and 6.4 show what percentage of parents identified each of eleven issues as some problem or a big problem. Table 6.3 shows results by private school, public school, and LSC parents. Table 6.4 shows results by race for the public school and LSC samples.

Safety issues. Respondents were questioned about four issues that related to safety: child's safety in the school, child's safety going to school, gang violence, and drugs. The general public school sample

Table 6.3

Percentages of Parents Identifying School Issues as a Problem, by Private School, Public School, and LSC Parents

	Private[a] (%)	*Public*[b] (%)	*LSC*[c] (%)
Child safety in school	3	30	18
Child safety out of school	14	45	38
Gang violence	4	48	26
Drugs	6	39	14
Poor achievement	9	49	44
High dropout rate	2	35	20
Education of non-English-speaking children	8	24	14
Education of low-income students	16	36	28
Resources	34	37	54
Parental say in school	32	53	42
Lack of parent involvement	41	60	90

[a] $n = 125$.
[b] $n = 253$.
[c] $n = 50$.

more often identified these four issues as problems than did the LSC parents or the private school parents. The difference is especially apparent with respect to the issues of gang violence and drugs—48 percent of public school parents felt gang violence was some problem or a big problem, whereas just 26 percent of LSC parents and 4 percent of private school parents felt the same.

In Table 6.4 more black and Hispanic LSC parents than white parents perceived children's safety in school and on the way to school as problems. However, LSC parents were less likely to identify other safety issues as problems in their schools than were other public school parents. For instance, whereas 40 percent of the general black public school sample felt drugs were a problem in their schools, just 17 percent of the black LSC parents felt the same. Hispanic parents were especially concerned with the issue of gang violence and drugs, with 58 percent of the general Hispanic public school sample saying

Table 6.4

Percentages of Parents Identifying School Issues as a Problem, Public School and LSC Parents, by Race

	General Public[a]			LSC[b]		
	Black (%)	White (%)	Hispanic (%)	Black (%)	White (%)	Hispanic (%)
Child safety in school	34	22	32	25	6	22
Child safety out of school	50	40	40	46	25	44
Gang violence	51	35	58	34	12	33
Drugs	40	33	47	17	12	11
Poor achievement	44	47	58	50	31	56
High dropout rate	37	19	49	21	19	22
Education of non-English-speaking children	17	28	34	17	0	33
Education of low-income students	46	15	40	34	12	44
Resources	46	34	49	58	50	44
Parental say in school	56	47	51	33	50	44
Lack of parent involvement	63	54	62	92	94	78

[a] Black n = 122, white n = 68, Hispanic n = 53.
[b] Black n = 24, white n = 16, Hispanic n = 9.

gang violence was a problem at their children's schools and 47 percent citing drugs as a problem.

Educational issues. In questions about education, parents were asked about poor student achievement, high dropout rate, educating non-English-speaking children, and educating low-income children. In Table 6.3 we see that public school parents more often identified each of these issues as a problem than did LSC parents or private school parents. There was little difference between LSC parents and other public school parents in identifying poor student achievement as a problem. But with respect to high dropout rate, and the education of non-English-speaking and low-income children, there was a greater difference. For instance, on the issue of high dropout rates, 35 percent of the general public school parents felt it was a problem, whereas just 20 percent of the LSC parents identified it as a problem.

Among public school parents, the major difference between parents in Table 6.4 is that more Hispanic parents, whether on the LSC or not, identified these educational issues as problems than did black or white parents. The only exception to this was on the education of low-income children, which black public school parents mentioned as a problem more than did other groups of parents. Black LSC parents felt that poor student achievement was more of a problem than did other black public school parents, but the black public school parents found a high dropout rate and the education of low-income children to be more of a problem than did the black LSC parents. The education of non-English-speaking children was thought to be a problem by more white and Hispanic public school parents than black parents, although no white LSC parents identified the education of non-English-speaking children as a problem. Black and Hispanic public school parents are more likely to see education of low-income children a problem than are white parents, and Hispanic LSC parents more often identified the education of low-income children as a problem than did their public school counterparts.

The lack of perceived problems with achievement and dropout rates is one of our most unexpected findings. According to accounts in the media, low achievement and high dropout rates are common problems in Chicago schools. Although public school minority parents found these areas to be more of a problem than did other parents, the number of parents who felt that these areas were problems was not as high as one might have assumed. For most educational issues, fewer than 50 percent of the parents identified them as problems.

Resources. Resources were broadly defined in this study as meaning funds, supplies, or personnel. Table 6.3 shows that LSC parents identified resources as a problem more often than did other parents. Thirty-four percent of private school parents, 37 percent of public school parents, and 54 percent of LSC parents felt they were a problem. Table 6.4 shows that black and white LSC parents felt resources were more of a problem than did black, white, or Hispanic public school parents in general. Given the funding difficulties that plague the Chicago public school system as a whole, the fact that fewer than half of the public school parents identify resources as a problem is surprising.

Parent involvement. Two issues were raised with respect to parent involvement in the schools: whether parents have enough say in the schools, and whether or not enough parents are involved. Table 6.3 shows that both issues were thought to be problems by a great number of public, private, and LSC parents. Ninety percent of the LSC parents identified lack of parent involvement as a problem in their school, and 60 percent of public school parents did the same. Private school parents also felt parent involvement was an important issue, with 32 percent saying parents did not have enough say in the schools and 41 percent stating lack of involvement as a problem. More public school parents identified a need for parent input as a problem (53 percent) than did private school parents (32 percent) or LSC parents (42 percent).

Compared to other public school parents by race, LSC parents, regardless of race, more often identified lack of parent involvement as a problem than did other public school parents. In Table 6.4 we see that over 90 percent of black and white LSC parents and over 75 percent of Hispanic LSC parents identified lack of parent involvement as a problem. However, fewer black and Hispanic LSC parents felt parental say in the schools was a problem than did black and Hispanic public school parents, and more white LSC parents than white public school parents thought it was a problem.

Educational Attitudes

Parents were also questioned about a variety of their educational attitudes having to do with parent involvement in the school, and their opinions indicate that parents do feel involvement is an essential part of the school. Parents were read a statement and asked whether they strongly agreed, somewhat agreed, somewhat disagreed, or strongly disagreed. Three statements had to do with the utility of parent involvement, and on these three statements parents overwhelmingly showed support for parent involvement.

The first statement was, "Parent involvement is important for a good school." Ninety-eight percent of the telephone survey parents agreed with this statement, as did 100 percent of the LSC parents. With the second statement, "Parent involvement is important for student success in learning and staying in school," 99 percent of the phone survey parents and all of the LSC parents agreed. And 97 percent of survey parents and 98 percent of LSC parents agreed with the

Table 6.5

Percentages of Parents Agreeing with Statements about Education,
by Private School, Public School, and LSC Parents

	Private[a] *(%)*	*Public*[b] *(%)*	*LSC*[c] *(%)*
Education is mostly the responsibility of the school	33	45	28
My school has an active and effective parent group	84	78	74
Parents at my school want to be more involved	61	65	56
Compared to other schools, this school is one where people get along well	89	81	86
I know more this year than I did last year about what my child is doing in school	78	73	84

[a] *n* = 125.
[b] *n* = 253.
[c] *n* = 50.

third statement, "Parent involvement can help teachers be more effective." Thus in overall school success, student achievement, and teaching, involvement was perceived to be an important ingredient by nearly all parents.

One statement we gave parents had to do with who had educational responsibility for children: "The education of children is mostly the responsibility of schools and teachers." Many parents somewhat or strongly disagreed with this statement, but in Table 6.5 we see that 33 percent of private school parents, 45 percent of public school parents, and 28 percent of LSC parents somewhat or strongly agreed with the statement. Table 6.6 shows that among public school parents alone, 49 percent of black and white parents and 24 percent of Hispanic parents agreed with the statement. By comparison, 33 percent of black LSC parents, 19 percent of white LSC parents, and 22 percent of Hispanic LSC parents agreed. Although the Chicago school reform has supposedly opened the schools to more parent input and responsibility, this question might indicate that parents still perceive few roles for themselves in the schooling process.

Table 6.6

Percentages of Parents Agreeing with Statements about Education,
Public School and LSC Parents, by Race

	Education is the School's Responsibility	Active Parent Group	Parents Want Involvement	People Get Along	Know More
Phone survey, public school parents					
Black[a] (%)	49	83	69	83	79
White[b] (%)	49	78	61	78	63
Hispanic[c] (%)	24	70	62	81	73
LSC parents					
Black[d] (%)	33	71	67	92	88
White[e] (%)	19	75	50	88	69
Hispanic[f] (%)	22	78	33	67	100

[a] $n = 122$.
[b] $n = 68$.
[c] $n = 53$.
[d] $n = 24$.
[e] $n = 16$.
[f] $n = 9$.

Two statements were asked regarding the current state of parent involvement at the respondent's school. Over 70 percent of all groups of parents agreed with the first statement, "This school has an active and effective parent organization." Private school parents were most likely to agree, LSC parents least likely. Among public school parents alone, black parents agreed more often than white or Hispanic parents; among LSC parents black parents agreed the least.

The second statement was, "Parents in my school want to be involved more than they are now at most grade levels." Given that "lack of parent involvement" was considered such a problem by parents, we expected that few parents would agree with this statement. However, 61 percent of private school parents, 65 percent of public school parents, and 56 percent of LSC parents agreed (Table 6.5). Table 6.6 shows that LSC parents of all racial groups were less likely to agree than were other public school parents. For instance, just

33 percent of Hispanic LSC parents agreed, but 62 percent of other Hispanic public school parents agreed. Apparently because they are the most highly involved, LSC parents are the most critical of other parents and their desire to be involved.

One statement that assessed school climate was, "Compared to other schools, this school is one where the principal, teachers, students, and parents get along very well." Over 80 percent of private, public, and LSC parents agreed with this. Hispanic LSC parents were the least likely to agree, and black LSC parents were the most likely to agree. The agreement levels for this statement suggest that parents are generally pleased with how teachers and staff work with parents and students in their own schools.

Finally, parents were asked to assess their own change with respect to their child's schooling with the statement: "I understand more this year than I did last year about what my child is being taught in school." Over 70 percent of all groups of parents agreed with this. Whereas 84 percent of LSC parents agreed, 73 percent of public school and 78 percent of private school parents agreed. Hispanic LSC parents in particular felt that they had gained an understanding in the last year—100 percent of the Hispanic LSC parent sample agreed with the statement.

Parent Involvement

In spite of the positive attitudes toward parent involvement, how are parents actually getting involved?

Getting involved at home. In one section of both the phone survey and the in-person interviews, we asked parents if they got involved in various ways with their child at home. A large majority of parents (generally over 80 percent), regardless of race, being from a public or private school, or serving on the LSC, reported that they got involved with their child at home. The one question (that did not constitute home involvement) where LSC parents and public school parents differed the most was on attending special events at their child's school. Nearly all (92 percent) LSC parents had attended a special event at their child's school in the last month. By contrast, just 49 percent of other public school parents reported attending an event. Even in the private school sample, just 69 percent had attended an event.

This question was included in the "home involvement" section because it was related more to a parent's involvement with his or her child than to the parent's involvement with the school. This result indicates that many parents find it difficult to physically go to the school. Parents in general seem to find it easy to do things such as help a child with homework, read to a child, or talk about the school day, but attending the school is less convenient and requires more planning and time than spontaneously getting involved with one's child at home.

Ironically, parent involvement in the home is more likely to improve student achievement (e.g., Leler 1983) than are other types of involvement. And yet many parents report that they are getting involved at home but find it difficult to attend a special event at school. In relation to the attitude that education is mostly the responsibility of schools and teachers, it would seem that parents perceive a split between home and school that is hard to bridge.

School involvement: Chicago parents in general. In examining parent involvement in the schools, we explicitly asked our telephone survey of 378 Chicago parents about their involvement in nine different activities: providing materials for the classroom, fund-raising, attending a meeting, observing children in the classroom, helping with a party, helping the teacher, volunteering in the cafeteria or playground or library, serving on a school committee, and serving as a school representative. In the in-person interviews of the LSC parents, we did not administer these questions but instead asked an open-ended question about past involvement.

Just 55 parents, or 14 percent of our sample, said they were not involved in any of the above activities. Table 6.7 lists the percentages of parents who took part in the nine activities, by race and socioeconomic status (SES); Table 6.8 lists percentages of involvement, by public or private school and grade level of child. As might be expected, private school parents, whites, and parents of elementary-school-aged children were generally more involved than were other parents. However, comparisons of involvement levels between parents on the basis of attending a public or private school, race, grade level, or SES generally varied by less than 10 percent.

In Table 6.7, although white parents tended to report more involvement than did black and Hispanic parents, the differences were

Table 6.7

Percentages of Parents Involved in School Activities, by Demographics

	All Parents[a] (%)	By Race			By Income	
		Black[b] (%)	White[c] (%)	Hispanic[d] (%)	Below $20K[e] (%)	Above $20K[f] (%)
Attend meetings	66	74	64	63	61	72
Fund-raise	56	56	67	36	43	67
Provide materials	38	43	34	40	33	43
Help teacher	35	36	40	29	31	39
Observe children	25	28	30	11	23	27
Help with party	24	19	29	26	21	27
Volunteer in library, etc.	14	15	17	7	11	16
Serve on school committee	14	12	22	6	6	20
Serve as school representative	7	9	6	7	7	8

[a] $n = 378$.
[b] $n = 148$.
[c] $n = 144$.
[d] $n = 70$.
[e] $n = 150$.
[f] $n = 215$.

usually minimal, especially between black and white parents. And, for a few activities, minority parents reported more involvement than did white parents. For instance, higher percentages of black and Hispanic parents than of white parents (34 percent) said they provided materials for the classroom (43 percent and 40 percent, respectively), and more black parents (74 percent) than white parents (64 percent) had attended a meeting in the last year.

Differences between parents from households of more than $20,000 and parents from households of less than $20,000 were also few. One of the greatest differences came on the question of serving on a school committee, where 20 percent of higher-income parents had participated, compared to 6 percent of lower-income parents. Higher-income parents were also more frequently involved in fund-

Table 6.8

Percentages of Parents Involved in School Activities, by School Variables

	Type of School		Grade Level	
	Public[a] *(%)*	*Private*[b] *(%)*	*Elementary*[c] *(%)*	*High School*[d] *(%)*
Attend meetings	63	74	74	51
Fund-raise	47	75	60	49
Provide materials	35	46	45	25
Help teacher	35	35	43	19
Observe children	22	30	29	17
Help with party	22	27	30	11
Volunteer in library, etc.	13	16	17	6
Serve on school committee	11	22	18	7
Serve as school representative	7	7	8	6

[a] $n = 253$.
[b] $n = 125$.
[c] $n = 251$.
[d] $n = 127$.

raising (67 percent) than were lower-income parents (43 percent). This finding might also be related to the fact that more higher-income families send their children to private schools, and private schools do more fund-raising than public schools do.

In Table 6.8, the largest difference in involvement between public and private school parents came in the activities of fund-raising and attending meetings. Seventy-five percent of private school parents reported helping with fund-raising activities, compared to just 47 percent of public school parents. This might be due to the fact that private schools rely on a variety of fund-raising activities and so provide more opportunities for involvement in this area. Additionally, 74 percent of private school parents, compared to 63 percent of public school parents, had attended a school meeting in the last year.

In all activities, elementary school parents were more involved than were high school parents. This was especially true with respect to activities that required parents to be in the classroom, such as volunteering in the school or helping the teacher. Even on the question of attending meetings at the school, 74 percent of elementary school parents, compared to 51 percent of high school parents, had attended. This is not an unusual finding; others have reported that involvement levels are much higher for parents of elementary school children than for parents of high school children (Epstein 1985; Stevenson and Baker 1987).

When parents reported involvement in a particular activity, we also inquired as to how they got involved in that activity. Parents most often reported that their involvement was activated by a teacher request. This was true regardless of race, age of child, or being from a public or a private school. One exception to this was volunteering in the school (in the library, playground, or cafeteria)—white parents and private school parents mostly got involved in this activity because the principal asked. Another important exception was serving on a school committee or serving as a school representative: Blacks and public school parents usually asked for this type of involvement, whites and private school parents usually got involved when asked by the principal.

School involvement: Local School Council parents. The fifty LSC parents were asked, "Were you involved in other school activities before running for the LSC?" in place of the yes/no questions used in the telephone survey. Of the LSC sample, 28 percent (n = 14) had never been involved in the schools prior to the LSC. Those parents who had been involved listed everything from daily volunteering in the school to occasionally helping out with fund-raisers as their involvement. Of the thirty-six parents who had been involved before the LSC, many were highly involved: seventeen of the parents (34 percent) had served as an officer on another school council, the local school improvement council, or the PTA, prior to the creation of the LSCs. By contrast, just 11 percent of the public school parents from the phone survey and just 22 percent of the private school parents had served on a school committee.

CONCLUSION

Overall, there were few major differences between the attitudes and perceptions of LSC parents and other public school parents. Private school parents on the whole were more satisfied and perceived fewer problems than did either the LSC parents or the other public school parents. However, LSC parents seemed to be more involved in their schools than were other parents.

In the area of satisfaction, although all parents had fairly high levels of satisfaction, LSC parents tended to be less satisfied in areas where they could be influential—such as school discipline, amount of time spent on reading and math, school cleanliness, and amount of afterschool activities. Perhaps this reflects their year of serving on the LSC, choosing which areas to focus their attention on and then, in turn, being most critical of those areas where they felt they could effect change.

Regardless of race, the LSC parents tended to be less satisfied than other public school parents. And both groups were less satisfied than private school parents. Often, black LSC parents were less satisfied than either white or Hispanic LSC parents. The biggest discrepancies in terms of satisfaction between the LSC parents and other public school parents were (1) black and white LSC parents were much less satisfied than other black and white public school parents in the areas of school policy and afterschool activities, (2) LSC parents were much more satisfied with school reform than were other public school parents, and (3) black LSC parents were more critical of the quality of teaching at their schools than was any other group of parents.

The first two findings might be the result of the parents' having served on the LSC. As suggested above, the LSC parents were probably most critical of those areas they perceived they could have an impact upon. And LSC parents would naturally be more satisfied with the reform than other public school parents because they felt a part of creating and implementing the reform. The third difference, of black LSC parents being less satisfied than other black parents with the quality of teaching, may be a result of many black LSC parents' having volunteered in the schools for many years before serving on the LSC. These parents had closer contact with teachers than did other groups of parents and were in a better position to judge the quality of teaching.

Generally, it is surprising that satisfaction levels tend to run as high as they do. It might be argued that the high levels of satisfaction are a result of the implementation of the Chicago school reform. On the other hand, it is possible that parent attitudes were positive to begin with and have never been as negative as critics and reformers have suggested; as Goodlad (1984) pointed out, other nationwide surveys have reported that parents tend to have higher levels of satisfaction when questioned specifically about their child's school as opposed to the quality of schooling in general. This seems to be the case with Chicago parents. In the eyes of the parents, the Chicago public schools are adequately educating their children.

As far as identifying problems in the schools, many parents were concerned with certain issues at their children's schools, though in areas such as student achievement, where an overwhelming number of parents might be expected to see problems, they did not. Whereas LSC parents were less satisfied with the schools than were other public school parents, with respect to identifying problems, the public school parents perceived more problems in the schools. This was especially true for black and Hispanic public school parents.

On the whole, however, these findings support the levels of satisfaction expressed by parents; apparently, parents do not perceive many issues to be major problems at their children's schools. The issue most often identified as a problem was not low achievement or safety, but parent involvement in the schools. This was identified as a problem by 41 percent of private school parents, 60 percent of public school parents, and 90 percent of LSC parents. Again, it would seem parents are most critical of this issue because they feel it is possible to make a difference through becoming involved.

Their attitudes expressed in this survey also suggest that parents believed involvement to be a crucial factor in school success. However, exactly what role that involvement should take is not clear. Parents seem to be unsure of the extent to which they are allowed responsibility in their children's education. And it is unclear exactly how parents wish to get involved. The view by many that education is mostly the responsibility of schools and teachers indicates that parents might be more willing to support the schools than to change them.

Involvement levels reflected this belief in parent involvement. In "home involvement" activities, such as helping a child with homework, LSC parents and other public school parents had similarly high levels of involvement. LSC parents were more involved than any other group of parents, public or private, in the activity of visiting the school. And more LSC parents than other parents in the phone survey had served on a school committee. Thus, it seems that those parents who are already involved in school activities continue their involvement through the LSC.

As for which model better accounts for parent motivations for involvement, the higher satisfaction levels tend to support the enablement model more than the empowerment model. But the fact that LSC parents were somewhat less satisfied than other parents offers some validity to the empowerment model. Although the differences were not significant, it is possible that had we gathered measures of satisfaction prior to their involvement they may have been significantly lower and may have been one reason these parents became involved in the Chicago school reform.

The parents' identification of problems also supported the enablement model. This was especially true for the LSC sample, who perceived fewer problems in the schools than did other public school parents. Minority parents, who identified more problems in their schools than did other parents, are one group that the reformers hope to empower by this reform. Yet it seems that although minority parents recognize some problems, they do not act on them as the empowerment model assumes. Rather than being spurred to change the schools, parents seem to take other courses of action.

Both models acknowledge parent involvement as an important factor in school success, and parents also express this belief. However, their involvement practices tend toward enablement activities rather than empowerment activities. This could be because the opportunity to participate in empowerment activities is rarer than the chance for enablement activities. In the next chapter we will look at how parents operated in an empowerment activity—the Chicago school reform. We study how the LSCs operated to understand how the parent interest manifested itself and what the consequences were of drawing the parents into school governance as formal representatives of parents and the community.

Chapter 7

Enablement or Empowerment?
The Workings of the Local School Council

Chapter 5, on the politics of the Chicago school reform passage, illustrated that the power of status quo-oriented politicians set the parameters for the reform and allowed only a very limited type of political architecture (Anderson 1979) to be erected, an architecture that designed parental input in ways that were congruent with the ideology of some of the reformers and supportive of both racial divisions and racial subordination. The ideology of empowerment legitimized the new design and cast it in a light that was acceptable to whites. It also undermined the growing power of black middle-class institutional interests and realigned the black poor with both business and reform strategies. These latter groups negotiated what reform was to be at the state level, trading concerns about funding for concerns about participation.

Once such scaffolding is erected, it can be used in many ways. Because the empowerment model specifies what parents want and how they want to relate to the schooling process, the actions of these parents in the new structures do little to change how the schools go about their business. This has as much to do with the goals and interests of the parents who have children in the public schools, and the people they select to represent them, as it does the political architecture that has been put in place by the political institutions of the state.

125

Much of the important work on race and schools has taken a more structural or institutional approach to understanding why African Americans are treated so poorly. Ogbu (1978) has used the concept of caste to argue persuasively that American schools are in the business not of offering equal opportunity, but of maintaining the racial hierarchy. While we are comfortable with this approach, the question we pose is, How is this hierarchy reproduced through increased parent participation? Our answer is that parents are, for the most part, not interested in exerting power over the school bureaucracies in ways that the empowerment model suggests. Most parents accept the authority arrangements implicit in the bureaucratic organization of the local school and see themselves assisting the professionals in the pursuit of traditional schooling goals. If this is the case, then the LSCs will not shift the power relations between professionals and parents. Indeed, the councils will support the power of professionals.

When we view this finding in the context of decentralization and the dispersal of power that it signifies, we see how the racial status quo is reproduced through participation and inclusion. Parents do not have goals for the schools and their children that differ appreciably from those of the teachers and principals. Even though there are areas of disagreement and conflict, most parents want the schools to be what the principals and teachers want them to be. Where serious disagreements exist, parents are at a distinct disadvantage in terms of the resources they can bring to bear. Time, money, and expertise are in short supply for most of the volunteers who serve on the councils. There are occasional changes in the quality of the teaching and organization at the schools, but these changes do little to redistribute the educational gains that African Americans receive as a caste within the larger context of the American economy and social structure. If parents and principals have congruent values and interests, little will shift in what the schools do and how they do it.

As noted in previous chapters, the Chicago school reform, utilizing an empowerment model, turned control of the system over to LSCs. Made up of a majority of parents, LSCs are responsible for setting school policy, approving budgets, and hiring principals. In October 1989, community members, teachers, and parents were elected to LSCs at each of the some 540 public schools. Using interviews with a random sample of fifty parents who were elected to their LSCs, we explore the question of whether reform necessarily leads to empowerment. For more information on the methodology and sample, see the Appendix.

FROM ENABLEMENT TO EMPOWERMENT

Although the enablement and empowerment models are distinct in their approaches and assumptions about parent involvement, some scholars think of them on a continuum of levels of involvement, with enablement being on one end and empowerment on another. Typically, empowerment activities are considered to be the apex of involvement (Bastian et al. 1986; Cervone and O'Leary 1982; McLaughlin and Shields 1987; Snider 1990). Parents also communicate this idea of some underlying ladder of activities that one must move through before participating at the empowerment level. The parents interviewed for this study expressed resentment when others who had not been involved previously were elected to the LSC. As one very active parent said, those parents "were never there for the real dirty work that nobody wants to do." Another parent spoke of her disappointment that other mothers who had been involved all along were not elected to the LSC—she felt they "deserved to more or less go on into the next phase" of parent involvement.

What happens when a system is set up for one model and forced into another? Each model suggests very different kinds of motivation for participation, and requires parents to develop disparate definitions of their role with respect to the school. In the enablement model, parents must think of themselves as augmenting the educational program of the school. In the empowerment model, parents set the educational program and must think of themselves as educational leaders. One model asks for cooperation from the parent, the other for assertiveness.

Although the Chicago school reform might not explicitly be about changing an enabled parent into an empowered parent, this transformation will be critical, given the traditional nature of the parent role in the school. In the past, the school system asked parents to participate in an enablement role, and now they are being asked to assume an empowerment role. How do you get from being an enabling parent to being an empowering parent? Essentially, this is what must take place in many schools, and we see that this hurdle is not easily overcome. Whereas a few parents became involved in the LSC thinking of themselves as empowered educational policy makers, most approached parent involvement from an enablement stance. The end result is confusion— what emerges is uncertainty as to what their role as parents in the schools should be, especially with respect to the LSC. Many parents began the reform process with little knowledge of the law or their duties, were frustrated by the lack of guidelines about their role in the schools, and groped to justify their position of authority.

Lightfoot (1978) wrote of the distinction between parents and schools as a separation of boundaries, with parents thought of as responsible for the socialization of children and schools responsible for their education. Present is not only Lightfoot's separation of boundaries, but also a *struggle over* those boundaries—where do parental rights and authority over the child end and the school's begin? The Chicago school reform is an attempt to force a modification of these boundaries by mandating authority to parents in a realm that is typically controlled by professionals. But although formal authority might be mandated, de facto authority cannot be, and parents must grapple with defining their role simply on the basis of a policy. "Empowerment" suggests an increase in power for the parent, but parents rarely possess the resources necessary to gain power in the schools. Parents are restricted by individual perceptions of what their role may be and by systemic constraints over what resources they have to do their job. Both restrictions limit their power and thus undermine their authority.

Furthermore, the act of including parents does not in itself solve problems in the school or change the traditional relationships between parents and schools. The creators of the Chicago school reform believed that having a majority of parents on the local school councils would lead to power for the parent. In an article about parent involvement, a reformer in Chicago says, "We felt that if parents had a majority on the councils, in practical terms, that would put them on about an equal par with educators" (Snider 1990, p. 17). But contrary to what the empowerment model and reformers would have us believe, parents are not necessarily unified in their vision. There is often a divisiveness among parents, based on education, race, and past involvement in the schools, that inhibits the power they might gain through being a majority. Morone (1990) discusses the key assumption that participatory democracy is based upon—a belief that the "people" to whom authority is given have a commonality in voice:

> [T]he usually implicit assumption is that the people agree with one another. The democratic ideal is founded on consensus. The people form a homogeneous body with a shared, discernible, public interest that transcends narrow individual concerns. (p. 6)

Morone suggests that this is a myth that has not been borne out in practice. And for the Chicago school reform, the reality is that without unity of voice and without the resources necessary to gain power, the parents' authority on the LSC is limited.

In an essay about participatory democracy and inclusion, Eckstein (1984) noted that, "Civic inclusion does change social institutions, but …it often changes only their 'content' not their 'form' (e.g., not elitism but the composition of elites)" (p. 140). School reform in Chicago does not change the fundamental relationship between parents and schools—it might include in the running of the schools a few extra people who happen to be parents, but it does not by itself alter the structure of education or the relationship between the school and the parent. Statutory inclusion in the schools mandates authority to the parents, but parents do not traditionally have a powerful role in the schools. Without altering the basic relationship between schools and families, moving from an enablement to an empowerment role for parents will be disruptive and difficult.

Reformers believe that changes in the law can shape the behaviors of school professionals and parents. But what we see through these interviews is that the individuals—the parents and the school professionals—shape how the policies work. The traditional relationship between families and schools, the typical role of the parent in the school, and the abilities and assumptions of the individuals involved are what define the Chicago school reform.

It should also be remembered that reform is being created within the bounds of an established bureaucracy. How much of the bureaucracy is open to change? Parents were brought into a bureaucratic system and became part of it. Much of what they learned was from the professionals and the school board. Thus in the case of the Chicago school reform, the empowerment model might also be implicitly creating legitimacy for the very structures parents are supposed to change. By being drawn into the governance of the school, parents are forced to be more involved in the existing system, and "the more active participants are, the greater the policy agreement will be" (Salisbury 1980, p. 6).

Although the parents in this study are dedicated to the spirit of the reform, besides being drawn into the system, they lack the information, time, or skills to produce any real change. Many of the parents spoke of a great deal of energy invested in simply working on the council, of the building of trust and of learning to work with a group. Parents were dependent on the knowledge and cooperation of the principal and teachers. Often, instead of using the LSCs as a new means of improvement, a new tool for reform, parents fell back on what they already knew and adopted a supportive enablement role.

·As for reform, parents declared their schools to be more open to their opinions; they felt that principals had to listen to them and that other teachers and parents felt freer to express themselves. This in itself is a worthy change, but will it result in educational change? By analogy, studies of the court system show that individuals are satisfied with the system when they feel they have been heard in a fair process, regardless of the outcome (Lind and Tyler 1988). Perhaps school reform will serve to make people more satisfied with the system by allowing them a voice in it.

Most parents are confused by the mismatch between their traditional supportive (enablement) role in the school and their new decision-making (empowerment) role. The factors that contribute to this general confusion are (a) personal and systemic limitations on what roles a parent may explore within the school, and (b) conflicts and struggles over status as each parent attempts to define his or her role and these parents clash with the school's traditional treatment of the parent. Many of these limitations would be expected in the first year of any new organization. But the conflicts of this first year may define the boundaries of LSCs and similar school reforms in the future. And that may mean that parents will have difficulty in ever truly taking on an empowerment role in the school.

In the end, as parents learned to cope with the conflicts and the limitations, individuals directed their energies toward the process of running the LSC—creating bylaws and running meetings. This is not atypical for bodies such as the LSC. In an analysis of community crime watch organizations, Lewis, Grant, and Rosenbaum (1988) found that the organizations were more concerned with process than with result. As they put it, "The way one does things outweighs the results of the process" (p. 28). Similarly, in the LSCs there is a focus on democratic proceduralism—people are hard-pressed to name results but are often able to talk about the process. Success meant consensus, getting along.

Perhaps the belief in process was a way for people to feel they at least learned what the system entailed, and consensus allowed parents to build an alliance with others on their council. But the process also gave parents a conviction that their voices were heard, regardless of whether the end result was far-reaching reform. This individual feeling of importance often does little to change the overall relationship between parents and schools or to fundamentally define a new role for the parent in the school. But it might allow parents to feel better about the school and about their relationship with the educational institution.

LIMITATIONS AND NARROWED DEFINITIONS

The authority provided through the school reform law actually contains few avenues by which parents can influence the school. Parents are not paid for their time, and the problem most often mentioned was a shortage of time to do all that was required. Parents often lacked the skills necessary to create a budget or suggest new curriculum. Training was one means by which parents could gain the needed skills, but the law provides little money for each LSC to get training. And with workshops given on a variety of topics and usually lasting just a few hours, parents had difficulty recalling what training they had received. One mother said, "It takes time to learn, because when they first give you read-out sheets you don't know what it is, and you don't know what goes with what."

The board of education provided training free of charge, but the one large training meeting for all councils was held in May, near the end of the school year, and focused on "boardsmanship"—group process skills—rather than concrete educational information. One mother stated, "Some of the training they're giving is not sufficient. A couple of people went to the boardsmanship training, which was worthless." In training done by many of the community organizations throughout Chicago, a running theme was the emphasis on group process and working to come to consensus.[1]

Furthermore, much of the information parents needed to do their job, such as information on costs involved in school improvements or guidelines for working with unions, was controlled by the board of education and the school principal, and so parents were dependent on the system for an important resource necessary to carry out their role. This created a relationship in which power was not easily transferred to the parent, and contributed to the ultimate confusion parents expressed about their role in the school.

That confusion was evident when parents spoke about not knowing what their role as an LSC member entailed. Parents believed their LSC role should have been clearly defined and were frustrated because they did not receive guidelines when they began the LSC. They blamed the board for failing to get the guidelines to them: "The board was late, even with the pamphlet saying what the LSC was all about." There was a clear expectation that the board should define their role and provide them guidelines; as one parent stated, "They were very slow in giving us information on how to function as a school council." Rather than creating their role on the LSC, parents wanted and expected definition of their role, just as they had received in their other enablement roles with the school. The irony is, should parents trust the board to give them guidelines when the board is the entity that the LSC was put in place to change?

A white mother from an upper-middle-class area of the North Side of Chicago described how the initial lack of guidelines caused problems for her council:

> [B]asically we were voted in and then not given a lot of direction in the beginning. So I feel like we spent a lot of time just spinning, spinning wheels. I don't think it was our fault that we were trying to figure out who were the leaders.

Similarly, another mother from the North Side described her disappointment that there was not better preparation for LSC members:

I had hoped that they would have it more together.... [T]here were too many times that we got information, "This is what's going to happen" a week later, "Oh no, that fell through." ...[If] you don't have the foundation set, where can you go from there? I mean, I thought we were coming in to like continue the growing part of local school councils, I've gotten the impression more than once that we're still trying to form the base of it. And it's frustrating.

There was a sense in this parent's statement, and in other parents, that they were there to help a grand experiment work, and that "others"—the board, teachers, the principal—should have been clearer about what the LSC would entail.

Parents thus began with a sense of not knowing what their role was, and they then met with other limitations. These were apparent when parents were asked about working on the school improvement plan and the budget, two of the most important duties of the LSCs. Training sessions about school reform provisions stressed that creating the school improvement plan was one of the most important powers of the LSC. The law states that, "The local school principal shall develop a school improvement plan in consultation with the local school council," and that the LSC will then approve the plan (Chicago School Reform 1988, p. 42). The budget was to be drawn up in a similar manner. Some LSCs created committees for the purpose of creating the plan and budget, but many others let the principal or the staff completely control the creation process and stepped in at the time of approval.

Although the law puts the principal in charge of the development of the plan and the budget, the LSC is given ultimate approval over the product. Yet in the end LSC members often had little input, because it was difficult for parents to know what they should be doing. Parents communicated that they were constrained by time and by their limited understanding of what was required. A white mother said:

[O]ur principal did most of it because we didn't know how to do it. We didn't know exactly what was supposed to be in it.... But it still went through, because we didn't have time. It was fast, and then the literature comes too late and then we have to have a special meeting, and it's due the next day. And then, I don't know, they extended it for another two weeks, and maybe if we had known that, we wouldn't have hurried it so fast, but anyway, he revised it. I mean I read it driving to work, all the highlights. And then I called him and said, "When you present this next week I will vote for it." So then when he presented it, it was unanimous.

Although this parent believed that changes could later be made to the plan and budget, at the moment of decision the lack of resources (the limits of time and information) allowed the principal to control two of the major duties of the LSC.

Similarly, one Hispanic mother discussed how her council trusted the teachers to construct the school improvement plan because the council lacked the knowledge to create it:

We had the teachers put up a rough draft. I mean, we trusted the teachers and we'd have never known how to do it.... [T]he teachers made a rough draft and if we needed something we went over it with him. You know, some of the parents wanted something included, they would tell the principal.

Another Hispanic mother described the process of approving their budget as one where the principal knew best:

[We made] most of those decisions according to the principal—she knew more than us what the school needed and where the money should go, so we just had to approve what she wanted to get done at the school.

Both of these mothers felt that the parents agreed with what was approved and probably got what they wanted into the school improvement plan and budget. However, the fact that the process is strongly controlled by the teachers and principal, with the parent voices as secondary, indicates how parents are limited to an enablement role with respect to the local school council. The amount of information these parents felt they needed in order to construct a school improvement plan and budget was massive. And in the face of deadlines, school staff were allowed to direct the process.

One parent whose council was controlled a great deal by the principal explained that he had not been allowed to see the budget. The principal was able to control the actions of many of the council members by suggesting what would be the best process in creating the budget. A white father said:

> [T]he council, at the principal's urging, put their entire authority in the school programmer, the assistant principal. Who then with the principal put [the budget] together. Not one council member, myself included, knows anything about what's in the budget right now.

In reality, parents had little choice but to trust the teachers and the principal. The principal had the advantage of resources and experience. Often parents became more aligned with the principal when she or he offered aid to parents rather than attempting to control the LSC. A black mother explained:

> You know, 'cause there were still a lot of things that we ran up against, that we had no knowledge of, and the principal, because she'd been in this school for almost fifteen years, she had been exposed to it, and she knew exactly what it meant, and she was able to explain a lot of things to us. And you know, she told us, if there's something you don't understand, I'll try to help you, or I'll recommend you to someone who can.

It's questionable how much input parents have on the LSC. The Chicago Panel on Public School Policy and Finance studied participation rates at LSC meetings for twelve schools (Easton et al. 1990). This study found that of all LSC members (except for student representatives on high school LSCs), parents (excluding the parent chairperson) were the least likely to speak in meetings. Furthermore, an analysis of the types of issues covered at LSC meetings in the first year showed a lack of focus on curriculum and school reform. Program issues (raised by the principal) and general LSC procedural issues were two of the most frequent topics of discussion. According to these findings, initial reform is superseded by the principal's domination and group process.

The parents we interviewed confirmed the Chicago Panel's findings. Because most parents typically have interacted in the school in an enablement role and because parents do not have the resources to experiment in an empowerment role, they continue to perceive that the principal is in control and that they are there to support his or her direction. One white mother from the Northwest Side of Chicago said she felt that the principal *should* control the budget and the school improvement plan process:

> [The principal] did most of the work because he really is the one who knows the most. And then we'd discuss it and improve, or give ideas or whatever. But he did most of it. Which is really what—how I think it should be anyway. I mean, I'm not about to start fooling with the budget. He would always ask us, but we would pretty much stick with what he had.... [S]ometimes people on the board felt they had to put their two cents in about something...when maybe the best person to handle a certain thing would have been just the principal.

Many parents might agree with this parent's position; however, the purpose of the reform was for parents to move beyond an "advisory" role in the school and have an active part in the school policy-making process. The approval of the LSC holds little weight if parents lack the information and resources necessary to make significant contributions to creating school policy.

It was not merely the very real constraints of time and information that parents were forced to overcome, but also the boundaries of their authority. The frustration with the board in failing to provide guidelines is one indication of the difficulty parents faced in determining their authority. Although guidelines put limits on the roles parents might conceive for themselves, without guidelines parents lacked any working model for their new empowerment role. The lack of time and information further narrowed parents' visions of ways they could be involved and many resorted to adopting an enablement stance.

Although the enablement role promotes consensus and causes the least amount of conflict, the enablement mind-set makes it difficult to adopt an empowerment role. And it is questionable whether the reform, which requires that LSC members be reelected every two years, is written so that the parent can gain the information and skills required to eventually assume an empowerment role. Such strict term limits are a major constraint, especially given the seeming lifetime tenure of school staff.

There are indications that some parents ignored or were able to overcome the inherent limitations on their power. This was the case for the parents who approached reform already empowered. We identified nine of the LSC parents we interviewed as empowered to begin with, and although they were still faced with many constraints, their approach to overcoming these personal and systemic limitations was different. Instead of leaning toward consensus and relying on the knowledge of the school staff, these people tended to question the process. One father told of how his council forced the principal to pay attention to them:

> I don't think [the principal] took it serious at first. But we did a power move on him—in one of our sessions we stopped all sports, all football, totally. They'd been working on this, but he didn't attend that session. So until we could evaluate the necessity of sports within the school and how much of the population they served, we stopped sports. Right after that he took us more seriously.

By asserting what power they did have, the council caused the principal to recognize their potential power, and the principal realized he had to listen to them. Few other councils were able to become united in such a manner—though this example does suggest the possible influence, toward order or chaos, the LSC might have.

Part of the ability to take on the empowerment role has to do with the expectations parents begin with. In contrast to the enabled parents, the empowered parents tended to have more concrete, realistic expectations about their new role. For example, some of the men who had not been involved in the schools before the reform stated they were prepared for the conflict and disorganization they would face as LSC members. One father viewed it as a political challenge: "[T]he legislature who initiated the program was predicting...that it would not succeed. And I like to make politicians fail when they make those kinds of predictions." Although these parents had not been involved before, their expectations allowed them to handle difficulties that arose in their LSCs and maintain their empowerment position. It might also be argued that these parents were unfamiliar with thinking of themselves in an enablement role and so more easily adopted their empowerment stance.

In ironic contrast, many of the parents who had previously been involved in the schools had few expectations of what they would be doing as an LSC member. A number of women who had volunteered at the school quite regularly said they really didn't know what to expect, whether a lot of time would be required or what decisions they would be involved in.

There appears to be some gender difference here—most of the parents who had clearly articulated expectations were men. But men were also least likely to have prior involvement in the schools. Those parents who had previous experience with the schools tended to be female parents. And so it is unclear whether the lack of expectations for enabled parents is related to their gender or their previous experience with the schools, or both. Either way, many parents who had a great deal of previous involvement in enablement activities lacked a clear perception of their empowerment role because they had so long been entrenched in an enablement role.

CONFLICT AND STATUS

The limitations placed upon parents was just one factor determining how parents adapted to the empowerment role. The other major factor was how individuals interacted with the other persons on their council. Individuals worked to stake out their own niches and develop opinions on issues they had never before considered. The process of developing opinions allowed parents to determine the important school issues. In an enablement role, parents are usually responding to the needs others define in their school. But in empowerment, parents had to learn to work with others in defining the issues. This seemed to be difficult for those parents who had always been involved. One young Hispanic mother who had always been involved in her school stated that participating in the LSC was much harder than she had expected because of having to learn how to function in a group:

> To get along with the other members on the LSC, to me that's hard. Because everybody wants to be chief there, and you know you can

only have one boss, and everybody's going, "No, no." We're always fighting, 'cause everybody's got some kind of idea. And the chief is like, "Well, this is good, this is good." And we're all fighting, that's what it is, one big fight.

This mother said that they fought about getting new desks or new curtains for the school, and that in the end "nobody got nothing." She said she hoped that in the future they would get the principal out of the school and she also wanted "to get new council members in there that are different. I don't like the ones that are working now." This woman felt that one person was "coaching" everyone else and would not listen to her ideas. Her LSC was defined by fighting over whose role would be important on the council, who would be listened to more than others. This parent also believed she was justified in her position, and that the other council members were wrong.

Other parents also communicated the correctness of their position and opinions in comparison to others on the council and expressed surprise at the "different ideas" or "hidden agendas" of some members. One Hispanic mother was angry at the number of outside interests affecting her LSC:

> [S]ome of the members on the LSC, they were trying to dominate, trying to run the whole show, trying to...make you do things the way they wanted you to...even though you believed it was wrong. And we had a lot of problems there, conflicts there, within the LSC itself.... [T]he people that wanted to be powerful, they wanted us to do what they wanted to do. If it meant not giving a person a chance, or even to listening to the other side, they wanted that person out.

The specific problem this mother was referring to was in rehiring the principal. Eventually, a majority of the council voted down the group that was trying to control the issue. But because of the difficulty in working together, a number of people on the LSC resigned.

Some parents ran for the council because they viewed themselves as having better intentions than other parents. One white father who had never been involved before spoke about his interest in protecting his son's gifted programs:

I wasn't sure what the extent of the authority of the LSC was going to have. And I saw the potential for—possible potential for—it to do harm instead of good. So I was really there to look out for my son's interests, specifically the gifted program.... I figured you could get a few nut cases on our council like that and they could start taking off in directions that wouldn't be productive.

Other parents who had been involved in the school a long time felt that others were not as qualified as they were to be on the LSC. Such parents were suspicious of why someone would suddenly get involved. One mother felt that those who ran but lost probably had personal motives for running: "[I]f your interest was for the kids, you would be still coming to those meetings." Another parent who was an officer on the PTA said that she ran on a slate with other PTA members to guarantee that the LSC would not be used for personal gain.

[B]asically the other people that I ran with, we felt that we didn't want people who were just in it for selfish reasons to win, and come in and start messing things up because they were just in it for political reasons or whatever. So more, it was sort of a protective measure against what I thought was a good school, and I didn't want other people who maybe didn't really care that much running it.... I didn't have any great things I wanted to do from it.

As individuals justified their position in relationship to others, parents often became aligned against the very people the reform was designed to unite: other parents. A white mother from the North Side talked about how she did not expect work on the LSC to be so "tough —sometimes you make enemies." She spoke of how the LSC parents were in conflict with the PTA parents:

There was a situation when we were writing up the bylaws. That took us a long time. We had two non-LSC parents which were also the president and treasurer of the PTA. And the rest of us, the other three of us or four of us were LSC members. And we were trying to write up the bylaws, and they kind of like had standoffs, because they wanted to be able to talk whenever they wanted. If we were discussing something they wanted to just like say whatever they want.

The issue was finally settled by outvoting the PTA people, so that they had to wait until the end of any meeting to be heard. This woman talked about the establishment of the rule for the sake of order, but it also pertained to defining who was in charge at the school, the LSC or the PTA. As this mother stated, in the past the principal only had to "bump" his ideas off of the PTA or the teachers, but the new LSC entity took attention away from the other parent group.

Many respondents echoed these conflicts with other parents, particularly with the PTA. One parent said her LSC "had people from the PTA resign as a result of the LSC coming into play." Another parent who had never been involved prior to the LSC said that he always had trouble with the PTA: "There was no way to become involved. The PTA was run to keep parents out." One Hispanic mother said that there was a lot of prejudice at her school that discouraged her from being involved in the PTA, a group primarily run by white parents. Instead she just volunteered in other ways: "I still went to school and I still volunteered anyways, but I just stayed away from those people." A few other parents suggested that the PTA was part of the problem in the schools or that they had become possessive of the power they had. Said one white father:

> Basically why I said I had to run was because I didn't want to see [the LSC] become another PTA. And unfortunately, half of the people on the council are PTA members.... It's controlled by the principal and the PTA. They can vote just about anything they want.

The traditional enablement role of the PTA is questioned when the additional empowerment role is offered at the school. While some PTA parents sought to become part of the LSC, others subtly undermined the LSC's authority. One parent spoke of how her LSC wanted to hire a computer coordinator to work with students, but that the PTA was against it because "they initiated that computer program, and they didn't want somebody from the outside coming in and running it."

Conflict was a means for parents to define their individual roles on the council. For those parents who were involved prior to the LSC, there was the personal conflict of justifying their past enablement role while trying to take on an empowerment role. Some involved parents who were not elected or chose not to run for the LSC might have sought to maintain and strengthen their positions in the school by aligning themselves against the LSC. And parents who had not been involved before could both justify their lack of prior involvement and define their empowerment position by conflicting with the PTA and other highly involved parents.

WHAT CHANGE?

Despite the conflicts, a good deal of emphasis was placed on trying to reach a consensus on the councils. Earlier, we cited Morone (1990), who noted that democratic participation was based on an assumption of consensus. Without consensus, the majority strength of the parents on the councils is lost. We attended some of the training sessions given by the community organization Designs for Change. One part of a session, "Ingredients of a Group That Works," listed factors that would help a group reach consensus (Chicago School Reform Training Task Force 1989). Many parents in this study said that the people on their council had all learned to work together. One white mother described how her council always agreed: "Well, we worked very well together on everything. I'm not kidding.... We have reached consensus on every single thing." Another black mother also said, "There was never anything we couldn't come together in agreement. We could still toss it about and hear the pros and cons and whatever, and then we'll make a unanimous decision."

Although the process of consensus may have helped the LSC to work more efficiently, it could be a time-consuming process. A white father expressed his frustration with the need to always reach a consensus:

[I]t became a very frustrating, a very ungratifying experience. And coming from business, I'm used to sitting in the room with one S.O.B. at the front of the table calling the shots. And you know, whether you like the person or not, you got things done. Here, I mean, you know, I don't work well in a group in terms of coming to consensus.

Also, due to the limitations on information, the focus on consensus put parent voices in a weaker position, where they were more likely to be subordinated to the interests of the school staff.

Furthermore, consensus sometimes resulted in inaction. For instance, when asked to talk about a specific occurrence that showed how her LSC worked together, a black mother at a high school related an incident where all the LSC members agreed not to get involved. The teachers came to the LSC asking that they determine a policy for dealing with student tardiness:

> What we decided was that if you're going to hire a principal, and have her have leadership, then the principal has to handle the day-to-day procedures. We can't get involved with, well, if this kid's tardy, what should be the punishment, and whatever. Unanimously, we all agreed that the day-to-day operations of the school should be allowed to be performed by the principal.

This statement also raises the question of what kind of problem *would* this LSC focus on? While reformers stressed that the LSC was a policy-making board, not a management board, we wonder what issues would be defined as policy and what as management.

The attention paid to consensus perhaps caused this parent, like others, to spend a lot of time describing the process by which her LSC reached a decision. She went into great detail about a retreat some members of her LSC went on, what they did on the retreat ("writing on big pieces of paper, taping them to the wall..."), and how she "really appreciated" the chance to "have a closer feel with our principal." She said she also learned that people in any position were important. Parents often detailed the process of learning how to get along and communicated a feeling that success was contained in the process. Because the LSC is mostly process rather than product, what do you describe, what is success, if not the ability to get along with others?

A typical answer to the question of how the LSC worked well together revolved around the creation of the bylaws and how everyone seemed to agree. Said a black mother:

> When we were getting our bylaws and stuff together, and the president she would set up dates and we would have a meeting every week until we got the bylaws and stuff straight, and so we did that. We worked good. It was fun, it was interesting, I enjoyed it.

Bylaws, getting along, and the process of the LSC were, understandably, very important to these parents. They were definite indicators of their role, and they placed a framework on what "being on the LSC" meant. The formality of bylaws, of following Robert's Rules of Order —these actions typically define a professional entity. They were also tangible guidelines that an LSC member could use to get others to recognize the LSC as an important school body. When there were major problems with the principal or other members of the LSC, it was often because the formality—the process—was in some way being undermined. Or when a member wanted to disrupt the LSC, it was most easily done by not recognizing formalities.

For example, one white parent felt that the LSC would make little difference, largely because so much time was spent on small issues. The issue he discussed had to do with the formality of how the meeting minutes were written up:

> We used to sit and argue—well, what happened was there was one individual on the council who was the secretary. And she began to have her own private agenda along with another member on the council that she was friends with. And what you saw after a while was that the notes, the minutes to the meetings, started becoming editorials. And since the minutes were public documents, I got into a lot of arguments regarding the minutes themselves. Which to me, in general, seems very petty just to talk about it.... [But] you have to do things to respond to what we see happening. And you lose sight of the bigger picture.

In another case the principal undermined the authority of the chairman, a white male, by failing to recognize his agenda, thus taking over the meeting.

> [I]n the March meeting, I prepared an agenda, in consultation with the principal, and in the March meeting he came in with my agenda with items scratched out, saying we weren't going to discuss those. At that point he got the majority of council members on his side. And that was the beginning of the end.

When the one area within the control of the parents—the formal process—went unrecognized or was undermined, parents were further frustrated in undertaking their empowerment role.

The process was sometimes used by the LSC to maintain their distance from other groups or members. LSC members were able to separate themselves from the PTA by controlling the amount of input the PTA had in the process. Another father, black, described how, to his disappointment, the LSC used the process to shut out other parents from policy making.

[T]here was an attempt by the council to restrict the time or the involvement of the parents in the actual meetings. They were given the first thirty minutes of each meeting. The parents would have time, but as far as policy making, they would have no input...otherwise [than] to engage in a gripe session that was not looked upon by the local school council as something meaningful.

In this case the process was used as a means of keeping parents in a separate, less meaningful role than that of the LSC.

Is the importance of process a by-product of the first year of reform, or a consequence of who is on these LSCs and how they are set up? When asked the question, "How has your school changed in the last year because of the LSC?" many parents were hard-pressed for an answer. As a mother put it, "That's the question that drives us all crazy.... [W]e've worked furiously, ferociously for one year, but what ways have the school changed at all?" One parent said the outer school doors were painted, and another mentioned buying yellow slickers for the crossing guards. Very few of the parents cited any policies they had put in place that might bring about change in the next few years. Instead, the major improvement parents perceived in their schools was related to process, a feeling that their opinion meant something.

Does having a voice make any kind of difference? If anything, it makes people feel better about the school. One Hispanic father spoke of how his daughter's friends told her to have him do something about the dress code for gym:

[M]y daughter's happy because all her friends know I'm on the local school council.... They told my daughter, "Well, tell your dad now that he's on the local school council, they should change the code, you know the dressing code. He should talk to the principal."... And we brought it up and they're going to change it. They're going to be able to use pants and shorts in the gym.... Well, it was nice, it was nice to know the kids, really, they want a lot of things—it was nice.

So although this reform might not fundamentally affect the relationships between the parent and the school, small changes are taking place, particularly in parental attitudes toward the school.

Parents had differing opinions over the utility of the LSC as a means of reform, and some of these differences were related to race and income. Many of the white middle-class parents perceived a lack of power and wondered how much difference the school reform would make:

It's hard to say what would have been accomplished without us there, it might have gone just as well without us.... I don't think any great thing has happened. I mean, we don't have that much power. I don't think we have as much as some people think we do. Our only real power as parents is to hire and fire the principal. Otherwise we're advisory. We have a principal that does like to cooperate and take things into account, but all in all it's up to him.

I thought they would have actually, more power than they have. In some areas they're very limited. I thought they would have power to control budgets more, enact swifter change, but the way it was set up and explained, it's not as powerful as I thought it would be. It doesn't have the power I thought it would have.

The frustration in how little his LSC had accomplished actually led one parent to say that his time would have been better spent with his son, at home. When asked what he had to give up, this father replied:

What did I have to give up? Time at home. I was doing it, in a sense, for my son. I was pissing away time there, I could have been at home with my son, helping him with his homework.

CONCLUSION

In the face of limitations, conflicts, and getting through the process, parents are still trying to determine what this empowerment role means. Many of the parents interviewed had been involved at their schools in some capacity prior to running for the LSC. Their activities were almost wholly enablement ones—volunteering in the classroom, helping with field trips, serving on the PTA. Parents used the term *volunteer parent* to describe their roles in the schools. This term suggests what it means to be involved in the school in enablement ways. When parents enter the school to be involved, their relationship to the school changes and they are perceived differently from other parents. She is no longer simply a parent who occasionally interacts with the school, but she is labeled a "volunteer" who is there to support whatever is going on at the school. It is difficult for parents who are used to playing an enablement role in the school to switch to an empowerment role. Not only must they begin to think of themselves differently, but others at the school must also perceive them in this new role.

The empowerment model brings parents into an existing school structure and forces parents to understand how to work within the system before allowing them to change it. As we have seen, this is one reason the empowerment model, as it is implemented in Chicago, is bound to flounder. Parents participating in the Chicago school reform entered into a highly structured bureaucracy and were given few means through which to gain power and authority. In the end, parents often fell back on their familiar roles with the school, ending up supporting existing school structures. Further, parents do not speak with one unified voice and one agreed-upon educational philosophy. The conflict among parents themselves is not easily resolved and impedes the effects of an empowerment model.

However, the enablement model fares no better, making broad assumptions about how parents "should" act and assuming the schools are functioning correctly. Many of the parents in this study had been involved in their schools in enablement activities prior to running for the LSC, and gave little thought to getting involved in this new activity. The enablement model limits parents to a supportive role with the schools, making it difficult for them to change how they interact with the schools. In implementing an empowerment model of parent involvement, policy makers must take into account the existing relationships between parents and schools.

While many parts of the schooling process may need changing, the family-school relationship is integral to future reform. Yet the place of the parent is neither to run the school nor to be subordinate to the existing structure. Instead some model must be developed where parents and schools collaborate in certain parts of the child's education. And rather than mandating a particular type of involvement, policy should set the tone and the stage for parents and schools to work together. As Elmore (1979–80) suggests:

> [I]t is not the policy or the policymaker that solves the problem, but someone with immediate proximity.... [P]olicy can direct individuals' attention toward a problem and provide them an occasion for the application of skill and judgment, but policy cannot itself solve problems. (p. 612)

Similarly, a policy such as the Chicago school reform does not solve the problems of the schools. And in this case, the policy offers little opportunity for addressing school problems and does not allow parents the "occasion for the application of skill and judgment." So much time on the LSC is spent in maintaining the process of working together that reform can be addressed only secondarily.

We, like others (Fine 1993; Hess 1991), recognize that there are many stories of LSCs doing well. But we also acknowledge the voices of the individuals involved in carrying out this policy, and the limitations we hear in their stories. We question when and how this most radical of decentralization policies will ignite into fundamental change.

Cohen (1978) wrote that "tinkering with political manifestations does not produce increases in community or family power. Instead, it simply weakens existing arrangements so that those who already have power—that is, professionals—acquire more" (p. 444). Is the ultimate result of these "political tinkerings" in Chicago an increase of power for the professionals? Intentionally or not, this appears to be the case. With the energy of parents spent on staking out and defining their new territory and with a limitation of resources, there is little opportunity for reform. The professionals gain power because parents often become entrenched in their limited duties or frustrated by the system, with their time spent on maintenance tasks rather than substantive educational changes. The reform first disperses power through the development of the LSCs. But given the congruence between the attitudes of the parent elites and the parent mass and the basically supportive nature of their attitudes, the very participation of the parents legitimizes the professionals' grip on policy making and school operations.

NOTE

1. One of the authors (Nakagawa) attended training sessions to become a "volunteer trainer" during the summer of 1989. These sessions were run by the community group Designs for Change.

Chapter 8

Individual Limits to Empowerment

As the Chicago school reform shifts power from the school administration to outside interests, the question of who is getting involved becomes crucial. The parents themselves, with their perceptions and attitudes and individual styles, will in great measure define what Chicago school reform is all about. The previous chapter documented how a variety of factors work to limit the effectiveness of an empowerment policy. This chapter is a more in-depth description of the parents participating in the LSCs and an attempt to understand, from the parents' perspective, why they participated. We find that most parents either are supportive of the professional domination in the policy-making process or have little interest in the bureaucratic warfare it would take to change the power relations.

Some parents' motivation for involvement fits the empowerment model, but a greater number of parents are accustomed to being involved in an enablement way and do not think in empowerment terms. Many who had in the past been involved in their schools perceived this reform as an extension of their other enablement school activities. Other parents understand this to be a new way to get involved but are not motivated by the pursuit of control that the empowerment model would suggest. Rather, they participate for more personal reasons.

In our interviews, we sought to discover the motivations of parents involved in LSCs and to classify the individuals along an enablement or empowerment continuum. Parents were asked to talk about how they got involved in the LSC, where their interest came from, if anyone asked them to get involved, and how involved they had been in other school activities or in training sessions on school reform. They were also asked about their expectations for the LSC, to describe how their LSC worked together, and how they felt they personally changed through their involvement. The questions were open-ended. For a description of the sample, see the Appendix.

We explored this data looking for characteristics that would distinguish types of parent participation. First we did a general classification, sorting parents into the categories "empowered" or "enabled." We classified parents as empowered when they fit the profile depicted in the empowerment literature. Empowered parents conveyed a sense that parents have "a legitimate role to play in the public schools" (Fantini, Gittell, and Magat 1970, p. 16). Empowered parents also expressed an idea that they were there to "add new forces to the institutional politics of schooling, to make school politics more participatory and more directed by the needs of the entire school community" (Bastian et al. 1986, p. 133). Of the fifty parents interviewed for this study, fewer than 20 percent (nine) expressed in empowerment terms their reason for involvement.

By contrast, enabled parents were identified as those people who expressed a sense of being in the school to provide "assistance in the area of academic improvement" (Nye 1989, p. 330). The enabled parents view themselves as *learning* about the school and offering input rather than forcing the school to acknowledge their voice. Although reformers believe that most parents are dissatisfied with the schools and thus are motivated to change what takes place in their child's school, we found that the majority of parents on the local school councils saw participation differently, from this enabled, positive, supportive stance. Over 80 percent (forty-one) of the parents in this study were categorized as such.

THE ENABLED PARENT

Many of the parents classified as enabled stated that they had been very involved in their children's schools prior to becoming part of the LSC. The involvement standard is a helpful variable by which to distinguish parents, because an implicit intent in this reform was to include parents who previously felt left out of the system. But is this new opportunity for involvement drawing new voices to the system? Just over 25 percent (thirteen) of the fifty LSC parents interviewed had never been involved in the schools. On this basis, few new voices are being added to the system. And yet the voices that are new tend to be empowered ones. In a simple breakdown of prior involvement, we found that those parents classified as enabled were more likely to have been involved in the past than were the empowered parents. Table 8.1 illustrates the differences.

As can be seen, the enabled parents were much more involved than were empowered parents prior to running for the LSC. Additionally, there were differences by gender and race. Just one of the previously uninvolved empowered parents was female. The three previously involved empowered parents were African American. Nearly all of the previously involved enabled parents were female.

High levels of prior involvement by the enablement parents contributed to their LSC participation. Many of these enabled parents were mothers who had been involved since their children first started school. Perhaps because of their former roles, it was difficult for them to characterize their new involvement as one of "running" the school, and they approached their job with their previous experience in mind. When these parents were asked to talk about how they got involved in

Table 8.1
Prior Involvement Levels by Enabled/Empowered

	Involved	*Not Involved*
Enabled	83% (34)	17% (7)
Empowered	33% (3)	67% (6)

Note. Enabled *n* = 41, empowered *n* = 9. Actual numbers are in parentheses.

the LSC, their first inclination was to speak about how they have always been involved: "Ever since my first two were over at school, I'd go over and help with parents...we would have fashion shows and different things for the school. And I've always been part of the school since they were little." Many parents justified their current involvement by speaking of their prior involvement. In doing so, they characterized it in enablement terms, using words such as *helping* and *volunteering* to describe their past activities. Often parents stated that they assisted in school activities "when they were asked." Most of these activities involved fund-raising activities or other tasks that supported the school.

The enabled parents saw their LSC involvement much like they approached their previous activity. Many simply perceived the LSC as another step in their parent involvement career. One mother said, "Well, I was involved in the PTA, so I decided why not take my chances." Another listed the fact that she had been on the PTA for eight years.

The enabled parents with prior involvement assumed that they *should* be a part of the LSC because they knew more about the school, the teachers, and the parents than did other, less involved parents. And the school professionals would reinforce this belief by asking the already involved parents to run for the LSC. Nearly half of the enabled parents mentioned that a teacher or a principal or some member of the school staff had asked them to run. Table 8.2 shows the differences between enabled and empowered parents in terms of whether they were asked to run for the LSC. Many of the enabled parents were asked by both school staff and other parents. Included in the "Asked by school staff" category were those parents who mentioned that at

Table 8.2
Asked to Run for the LSC, by Enabled and Empowered

	Asked by School Staff	*Asked by Other*	*Not Asked*
Enabled	49% (20)	29% (12)	22% (9)
Empowered	11% (1)	33% (3)	56% (5)

Note. Enabled $n = 41$, empowered $n = 9$. Actual numbers are in parentheses.

least one of the people who asked them to run was a teacher, principal, counselor, or teacher's aide. Included in the "Asked by other" category were those parents who stated that someone other than school personnel asked them to run, such as friends, other parents, a child, or a community member.

Whereas the enabled parents were much more likely to be asked by someone at the school, empowered parents were more likely to decide to run of their own accord. In part, this factor also limited the enabled parents to a support role. By being asked to run by school staff, the message sent to enabled parents was that they were being invited into the school by the "professionals" in charge. Implicitly, this may have conveyed the sense that the parents were there to work with the staff; it must be difficult to develop an empowerment mind-set when the people you are to set policy for are also the people who helped you to get elected. Persons who are supposed to "take over" an organization are rarely invited in by the current bureaucracy.

Additionally, by being asked to serve on the council, the involved parents were not forced into thinking about why they should choose to participate in the LSC, or even to consider what the LSC entailed. And so these typically involved parents usually did not mention school decision making as a type of involvement that they were hoping for and did not capture the empowerment mind-set. Neither did they think of it as the "meaningful" parent involvement that reformers and researchers frequently characterize it as. For the most part, the enabled parent accepted her or his role in the LSC as another activity to support the school. One black mother who had a good deal of prior involvement in the schools talked about how she had "heard we were going to get in there and change the schools" but then realized that "wasn't going to happen." She said that she felt that, instead, parents were there to "make sure" things get done and to "basically help the school."

The theme of supporting the school might be related to parents' perceptions of their abilities to govern the school. Many parents, both enabled and empowered, mentioned that they had gained knowledge and confidence through their involvement in the LSC. A black father answered:

Did I gain anything for me myself personally? Sure, I learned, I think I learned a lot about the system. I also learned about the things that we had the right to do, to be able to help the system.

In Table 8.3 we find that over 25 percent (eleven) of enabled parents and just 11 percent (one) of the empowered parents felt that how they changed in being part of the LSC was by learning more about the system and the workings of the school.

As the father's response above illustrates, enabled parents often thought of what they learned as a means of helping the system. For the one empowered parent who felt he had learned a lot, knowledge meant more difficulty: the more he knew, the harder he found it to make changes. Similar percentages of enabled and empowered parents felt they had gained self-confidence through their involvement, although the enabled parents tended to state that they gained confidence and therefore could "speak out" or "feel proud," whereas the empowered parent viewed the change as "becoming more of a leader." Within the "Other" category were gains ranging from "sympathized with teachers more" (for the enabled parents) to "gained insight into ineffectiveness of the system" (for the empowered parents).

Just as there were varied perceptions of how parents felt they had changed through their involvement, there were also many sources for parents' interest. Table 8.4 categorizes some of these interests.

"Children" was a common theme for the enabled parents. Twenty (49 percent) of these parents often mentioned general hopes they held for children, from which their interest arose. In comparison, just one of the empowered parents mentioned children as the reason for

Table 8.3
How Parent Has Changed through LSC Involvement

	Gained Knowledge	Gained Self-Confidence	Gained Other	No Change
Enabled	27% (11)	24% (10)	39% (16)	10% (4)
Empowered	11% (1)	22% (2)	44% (4)	22% (2)

Note. Enabled $n = 41$, empowered $n = 9$. Actual numbers are in parentheses.

Table 8.4
Parent Interest in Becoming Involved in the LSC

	Children	*Help Out*	*Prior Involvement*	*Concrete Reason*	*Other*
Enabled	49% (20)	12% (5)	17% (7)	20% (8)	2% (1)
Empowered	11% (1)	0%	0%	78% (7)	11% (1)

Note. Enabled *n* = 41, empowered *n* = 9. Actual numbers are in parentheses.

involvement. The enabled parents often discussed children in general, speaking in impressionistic terms about parent involvement. One white mother from an upper-middle-class area of the North Side discussed her priorities:

[T]he things that I feel are important are I would like the type of discipline or the way that children are viewed at the school in a more positive light, rather than with pessimism or with negativism.

Another black mother from the more working-class West Side said her interest in the LSC came from her concern "for the welfare of all the children...trying to find ways...to help all low achievers achieve and make themselves feel good about themselves."

Related to the focus on children, there is a sense of protection expressed by many of the enabled mothers, a feeling that they need to watch over their children and could do so through involvement in the school. The mothers who tended to discuss their involvement in these terms were often African American. As one African American mother from the South Side said:

Since my kids were in kindergarten I've been involved. I'm very concerned about my kids, and I don't like nobody showing things to them. That's my concern, just to make sure it's done right, the way I would do it.

The mother's concern with watching over her children may have arisen from the feeling that another respondent expressed—an idea that the teachers, who were not from the neighborhood, did not understand their children:

> We had teachers in the school who had a nervous breakdown, they can't deal with the pressure.... Black kids are pressure. They love putting pressure on you and they do things to aggravate you just for the hell of it. And if they can't take the pressure, then let them go to another school. Because the kids know when something is wrong with you. And like I told her [principal], "you might say I'm prejudiced but that teacher cannot deal with these kids."

Although it might seem that the notion that parent involvement represents protection might translate into empowerment, this is not the case. These mothers justified their involvement in terms of watching over their children, but this did not mean that their involvement also had to be aimed at specific improvements to the school. These mothers felt their *presence* in the school was enough to ensure their child's well-being. Thus, the way the mothers discussed both their involvement in the LSC and their past involvement was through enablement terms—it was to help their children, not to change the system.

As shown in Table 8.4, about 20 percent (eight) of the enabled parents did not mention children as their interest for involvement, but were more concrete in their reasons for being involved (in contrast to the empowerment parents, where 78 percent had concrete reasons for their involvement). Often these enabled parents discussed specific skills they could offer to the council: "I thought I could help the council because I have a strong secretarial background." Other people had specific reasons, sometimes similar to the empowerment ideas, for why they should run for the council. One Asian mother said her interest in running came from a concern for minority representation:

> [W]hat got me thinking was that they were saying that the people who should run for the LSC or serve on the LSC should reflect the school community. And it's always been sort of a stereotype that Asians, and more specifically Chinese, do not get involved.... And so I decided, well maybe I should do it.... I thought I should at least have a Chinese name running.

Whereas many of the enabled parents took it for granted that they should participate in this LSC activity, some believed that other parents were not as qualified or would not be interested in running. One white mother from the North Side expressed this belief in talking about why she got involved:

> I was originally involved in the PTA and basically there were only a handful of people that were active. And we sort of said, "Well, let's run for this thing," thinking no one would be interested, because no one had ever been interested in anything that went on before.

Similarly, another white mother from the North Side stated her feeling that others did not have the credentials she had for running: "I really felt that nobody else that ran, except my friend...knew as much as the two of us about school-based management."

These parents were finally classified as enabled because they did not view themselves as truly having policy control in school management. They still discussed their role on the LSC in terms of "helping" the school and had few expectations for how the council should run. The mother who ran with other members of her PTA was unsure if things at the school would have changed much without the LSC: "It might have gone just as well without us." She also felt that the changes they made were small ones, and that for the next year the council "has a little bit better understanding of what the school needs." The parent who ran for the LSC in order for the Asian population to be represented felt that it would "be kind of exciting" to be on the LSC and felt that the school was already running pretty well. Perhaps these parents are at a transitional stage between enablement and empowerment, where they appreciate having more of a voice in the system but are unsure of how to deal with this role. They tend to fall back on what they know and maintain a certain level of satisfaction with how the system functions.

At the beginning of this section, we found that many of the enabled parents had previous involvement with the school, whereas the empowered parents tended to have no previous involvement. However, there were those enabled parents (seven) who were not involved at all prior to the LSC. Primarily, their reason for no previous involvement was that they had not had the time. It might seem that not being involved in the past might force these parents to be more articulate in their reasons for participating now, because they are unable to fall back on their prior roles. But their reasons for participating were vague and tended to center on involvement's being "a good thing to do" or their wanting "to see what was going on in the schools." One Hispanic mother who had been a teacher in Mexico talked about her interest in the LSC:

> When the news started coming out about the new reform, I thought that I wanted to be about the school because it's something that I liked to do.... [T]he parents, they should be helping the teachers because we cannot expect everything from the teachers. We have to help our kids, you know, and give them the most support to them in order to learn, in order to accomplish what they are for.

This parent expressed enablement ideas in her perceptions of parent involvement as a way of supporting the school and helping the teachers. She felt that if the parents would "be involved 100 percent" then "the kids they...will do perfect." Similarly, a black father who stated that he was not involved in anything prior to the LSC cited helping his children as his reason for being involved:

> I have children in the system, and I would like the system to be the best that it could be. Any kind of help that I can give to them, I'm willing and prepared to give them.

THE EMPOWERED PARENT

As noted earlier, the empowered parents were primarily uninvolved parents who, in contrast to the enabled parents, did not view being on the LSC as an obvious next step to take. Perhaps because of their lack of prior involvement, they cited explicit reasons for becoming involved and demonstrated a very conscious decision to participate. Their purpose for involvement, their intent, was thus more considered than for the enabled parent. Said a black father:

Well, I got involved based upon my child's going to the school. I wanted to be a part of the reform process that I thought manifested itself in the administration of the local school council.

Said a white father:

[T]here's an article in the *Chicago Tribune* about my school's principal refusing to reveal the names of candidates. There's the inference by the *Tribune* writer that the election was being rigged, which—as it turned out—was true for the two community candidates. After reading that I decided to become a candidate.

These empowered parents were often critical of the parents who had typically been involved, viewing them as part of the past problem in the school. As one father said, "The PTA seemed more or less to belong to the program—the same problems were still there." One black mother who had no prior involvement expressed a similar view about parents on her LSC who had a lot of prior involvement:

One thing we should have realized...is that they had been involved in the school, and that itself should have told you that they were part of the problem, not the solution. We didn't realize that until we had gotten together as a council. They were part of the reason things had gotten so bad in the first place. They were some of the same people who were going along with the program of the principal. So we immediately come in battling with them because they're content with the way things are, we know that this isn't the way things should be.

This viewpoint is especially enlightening in view of the fact that enabled parents were often most suspicious of those parents who had never been involved before being an LSC member.

These empowered parents were also fairly confident of their abilities and rights as LSC members and entered into the process with an awareness of what being on the LSC would mean. One white father from the North Side spoke of his abilities:

I knew that I could function well within this type of setting.... I had some experience in the Catholic grade school, they had what's called local school boards, same thing. I served three years as chairman of a small grade school.

Another black father with no previous involvement in the school said he anticipated all the difficulties he found on the LSC:

> I was not surprised with anything that I encountered. I expected everything, the disunity, the fights, and the parents who felt left out of the process.

Other fathers spoke of the powers the LSC had, often citing the specific powers, and sometimes expressed disappointment that they didn't have more power. One father mentioned that if they took away the LSC's ability to hire and fire the principal, the LSC would have no authority at all. One white father from the North Side stated, "The only thing we had the power over for, was to approve expenditures that might come up from the teachers' requests for funds. That became a rubber stamp, that was a joke."

In contrast to many of the enabled parents who spoke in general terms about helping children to achieve, the empowered parents came across as more agenda-driven than other parents. They had precise goals in mind for what the LSC could accomplish, in comparison to the more impressionistic interests of the enabled parents. A white father from the North Side cited his goals for the LSC:

> When I first came in, there was two things I wanted to attack, one was security and one was curriculum. And I feel that every child deserves a secure environment to learn in.... [O]ne teacher [and] the principal felt they didn't have a security problem. Because of incidents that had happened in the school it was glaring that they had a serious security problem.

This incident was settled by the principal and teachers admitting that there was a security problem, and then the LSC was able to take action against it.

Three of the empowered parents had a lot of prior involvement and definite reasons for their involvement. These were parents who clearly fulfilled the assumptions of the empowerment model, and when asked to talk about how they got involved in the LSC they said that they had been involved in the school reform movement. Said a black mother, "I worked to bring about the school reform. I was one of those parents that schlepped their way up to Springfield." Said a black father, "I'm just involved. I was involved with helping formulate some of the reform legislation."

Whereas many of the enabled involved parents proudly stated that school personnel had asked them to run for the LSC, when questioned about whether someone had asked her to run, one empowered black mother was indignant:

> I would have been offended if someone had come out and asked me. It's just like when I go up to the school and they say, "Oh, you're here, isn't that nice." Well where in the hell am I supposed to be? It's just like if your child is hit by a car and you run out there to see what's wrong with him and they say, "Oh, it's so nice of you to come." Well what are you talking about?

This empowered mother was pleased with the work her LSC had done and stated that she was "satisfied" with how the reform was going in her school, but felt they still needed to put more emphasis on "what education is and what it's supposed to be." She was also for empowering the students: "The students have to be heard.... Our students have not learned to be active students, they simply regurgitate what the teacher said."

These three empowered parents who were previously involved were all black and middle-class. Two of the three were fathers, and both fathers mentioned an interest in running for alderman. This extension of the LSC role into politics indicates a sense of a civic duty being fulfilled through their involvement. The black mother was intent on explaining why she was an involved parent, and her wording resonated with feelings of civil rights:

> I often grapple with the question of why some parents are active and some aren't, and what makes some focus in on their children and their academic studies and struggles. And as for myself it comes out of my Southern background. I remember when I was very young, and my parents told me that it was not intended for black people here in the

United States to be educated, and during slavery times if you learned how to write they'd cut off two of your fingers, if you learned how to read your tongue would be cut out.... And so I learned that education was our salvation, at least that's what I still believe in.

These parents were not necessarily different from the typically involved enabled parent in their approach to reforming the school, that is, they did not always have a specific agenda in mind when they discussed what they expected from the LSC. Yet these parents consciously separated themselves from other parents when they discussed involvement. They suggested that they understood what involvement entailed, but that other parents were still learning. For example, one black father spoke about his LSC as if he were an outsider:

I think that this first year...you have to learn. You have to know what it is you want to do.... I think that mainly, what they have learned is you need six votes to pass anything so you learn how to work with people.

This distancing from other parents is probably a function of their belief that being involved with the schools is about learning how to function politically, and the already empowered parents have already learned how to do so.

For these involved, empowered parents, the reasons for being involved might best be summed up by the statement of one father discussing why he became involved: "The real question is why aren't they [other parents] involved, not why am I. Isn't that my responsibility?"

CONCLUSION

This analysis of LSC parents indicates that the majority of parents on the LSCs are not reform-oriented people. Of course, there might be a self-selection problem in that the parents who chose to speak with us were more likely to be enabled. However, one would expect the opposite to be true, that more outspoken, empowered parents would be more willing to speak about their experiences.

There is a particular "gender difference" in that the empowered parents are almost wholly male, and many of them are white males. Many of these fathers had a certain "systems" perspective, where they were able to look at many aspects of a situation from a big picture. This thinking in some ways embodies the empowerment model, which requires parents to have a systems perspective of the school. In contrast, women tend to take a community view, and the women in this sample tended to focus on their family and immediate community. Clearly, these gender differences are expressed in this analysis. And perhaps the rhetoric of reform is one of a male voice rather than a female voice.

If this sample is representative of the LSC parent population, then when parents enter into a policy position designed to empower, they rarely do so with the mind-set of changing the school. The empowerment model assumes that parents will accept the reform agenda, whereas most parents in this sample approached their LSC position with an attitude typical of the enablement model—they believed they would be learning how to help the school.

Other researchers also believe that the role parents desire in the school is collaborative rather than conflictual. Epstein (1993) writes, "...*power, authority,* and *control.* These are not the words that most parents use when they express how they want to be involved in their children's education" (p. 715). Epstein (1993) and Wasley (1993) note that parents want "information, communication, and participation" that will help their children to do better in school. In light of this, our findings are not surprising—one would expect that those who were involved before would be involved again, and that teachers would ask certain parents to run for the LSC—but what they point out is that a policy of decentralization is, ultimately, shaped by the individuals involved. And the plan for true educational reform through empowerment seems a tenuous hope.

At worst, an empowerment policy further solidifies racial differences and inequalities. Charles Hamilton (1969) wrote of the educational reform movement as a difference between black and white perceptions of the system. Blacks saw the problems of education through the lens of legitimacy, whites believed education problems were ones of efficacy. The attitudes expressed by the parents participating in the Chicago school reform still focus on legitimacy and effectiveness, but it is now black parents who call for effectiveness and whites who worry about legitimacy: In our interviews, many of the empowered parents who questioned the legitimacy of the system were white, and many of the enabled parents who wished to help the system run more effectively were black. With a majority of the children attending urban public schools being minorities, and with many of the top administrators also being minorities, whites are now using the issue of legitimacy, in contradistinction to the position of blacks.

Has decentralization legitimized public schools for minorities? One underpinning of the Chicago school reform is that the schools have been systematically closed off from the community. Yet if minority parents do not approach this reform with these concerns, we will see changes that are geared toward making the system more "effective" but not radically different. As evidenced by our sample, whites are comfortable with the notion of parent power in the decision-making process. The result is something quite different from what the architects of the reform imagined at the grassroots. It is of course possible that as the parents get more experienced in the new policy environments they will change their attitudes and assert their imputed interests more decisively, but the push for more power is not coming from the poor, minority parents; it is coming from the whites with a more middle-class agenda. What time might bring is further division between the schools already doing well and the bulk of the schools that serve the inner city. Ironically, participation may serve to widen the gap between the races, both within the Chicago system and statewide. When parent participation displaces redistribution as the policy objective, the result may reproduce the racial status quo.

Chapter 9

Conclusion

The argument we have made in this book is that school decentralization has reached the urban policy agenda because it reduces tensions in society. It allows the disadvantaged a voice in governance while it preserves the status of the elite. It offers a hope of change, but maintains the economic and political advantages of those in power. Decentralization can be a powerful policy for resolving urban conflict. But as Katznelson (1981) has pointed out, this kind of resolution imposes a silence that hides the foundations of that conflict, a foundation built on issues of race and class. To understand why we decentralized urban public schools, we must frame this policy in its political and economic context.

Toward this end we have argued that the decentralization of big-city schools incorporates and co-opts the demand for educational improvement into the bureaucracy. Rather than resolving issues of race and class, decentralization has masked these issues in inclusionary policies. But, as Eckstein (1984) noted, "Inclusion does not much make groups equal; rather, substantial equalization of the conditions of life seems to be the prerequisite for inclusion to work as intended" (p. 140).

By selecting five of the largest school systems in the country and analyzing the paths they have taken to decentralization over the last two decades, we sought to understand the political processes that are at work in producing decentralization in urban education. We found two different "types" of decentralization, enablement and empowerment. The type of decentralization implemented depended upon the politics at work in the city as a whole. The decentralization processes in New York City and Detroit create a picture of how racial conflict results in empowerment strategies for decentralization. In contrast, Los Angeles and Dade County, two systems that underwent decentralization more recently, utilized enablement strategies. Without a coherent "outsider" voice, these systems used the deinstitutionalization rhetoric to control the type of decentralization implemented. Rather than being placed in the hands of the community, decentralization powers were placed in the hands of the professionals.

We have stressed that, regardless of the kind of decentralization implemented, the ultimate result is a policy that does little to correct inequities in the system. We used the case of Chicago to detail exactly how this takes place. After Illinois state legislators made it clear that no new funding would be budgeted for what was touted as the most far-reaching school reform in the nation, the reform came to stand for process rather than outcome. There are those who believe that success will come from process alone. But to date there is scarce evidence to support this view. Our data suggest that, even if reformers alter the indicia of success to equal simply community participation, the Chicago school reform falls short—because participation alone has not led to empowerment in any real terms. We found that the reform shifts merely the appearance of control to the new participants; that it ensures that the balance of information power stays firmly with the traditional elites; and that it does not guarantee an effective hearing for a multitude of outside voices but, rather, transforms those outsiders into mere bureaucratic operatives—who, instead of taking aim at an inefficient monolith, snipe at mid-level bureaucrats. And in many cases these bureaucrats, like the new participants, are African Americans.

By turning the problem of education into a resolution of bureaucratic and democratic tensions, reformers claim that the solution to urban education is participation. As we have shown, the use of decentralization in the 1980s dispersed authority—but this was authority that middle-class blacks had gained in many urban school bureaucracies. In the case of Chicago, the result was a split between black middle-class school personnel and black lower-class parents. Reform groups, many led by white middle-class males, defined the issues for this community.

Banfield and Wilson (1963) described this more than thirty years ago, when they wrote of how middle-class definitions of urban problems began to dominate city politics. They saw reform agendas replacing political machines. Nonpolitical proceduralism was the mode of operation and benefited the middle-class professional. Still, they could not foresee how that reform mentality was to shape racial conflicts and transform them into issues of bureaucratic process. This new political architecture (Anderson 1979) established the priorities for a new generation of urban educators and community activists.

Politically, school decentralization accommodates the demands of African Americans while legitimizing government institutions of the majority. Yet the means by which the demands are met are shaped by the larger political culture and the efforts of groups outside the African American community. To understand this process we have looked beyond the dominant pluralist and radical models of urban politics from the last two decades. Today, national and local elites are confronted with the erosion of confidence in both bureaucratic and democratic solutions. Government itself has lost authority. Conflicts based on class and race have driven urban politics since the birth of the republic but, coupled with changes in the urban economy and demography, these conflicts must be resolved in new ways.

Decentralization is an ideology that, in innovative ways, represents group interests and draws groups into governing coalitions. These innovations change the nature of societal and governmental relations. Katznelson's (1981) insightful discussion of New York treats the ideology of decentralization as a form of false consciousness, a misreading by the poor of what was in their best interest. With the benefit of another decade of hindsight, we read the ideology differently, from an "interest representation" approach (Clarke 1986). Whereas reformers purport to represent minority parents and communities, the actual politics of the decentralization effort end up as an interplay between reform organizations and conventional political groups, rather than representation of class interests.

How was incorporation designed and with what consequences for the representation of interests in the decentralized system? We found that reform organizations played an important role in the design of the agenda for change and the definition of the problems. Strong reform organizations resulted in empowerment strategies. Where reform organizations were absent, unions and school administrators defined the nature of decentralization, resulting in enablement strategies.

Enablement decentralization strategies, guided by school districts, allow little room for parent and community interests. This lack of interest representation is a double-edged sword—it allows the district a freer hand in making policy, but it excludes poor, minority groups from any substantive participation in the decision-making process. But even empowerment strategies, purportedly representing the interests of parents and community, merely institutionalize these outside voices, filtering them through the prism of middle-class democratic proceduralism. The *expression* of parent interests—rather than their realization—is a goal in and of itself. In the five systems we studied, we found the continuing evolution of representation of new interests within government entities. Both approaches to the advent of school decentralization reflect major shifts in class and racial politics in urban areas, first defining, and then absorbing, parent and community interest groups into public bureaucratic structures.

Other scholars have also noted that decentralization allows more participation but does little to alter the system substantially. In a study of school-based management councils, Malen and Ogawa (1988) found that parents involved on the councils primarily supported the system rather than changed it. And in the 1970s, Ravitch and Grant (1975) concluded that decentralization in both New York and Detroit did not improve schools but merely allowed more individuals to participate. Although decentralization in its newest Chicago-style fashion is said to be different, our findings suggest that even this most radical reform again answers the call for democracy more than the need for school quality.

A CONSERVATIVE RHETORIC

The question remains as to the appeal of decentralization for reforming the schools. Derrick Bell (1992) believes that policies that directly threaten the status quo of whites will never be fully implemented. He concludes:

> The goal of racial equality is, while comforting to many whites, more illusory than real for blacks. For too long, we have worked for substantive reform, then settled for weakly worded and poorly enforced legislations, indeterminate judicial decisions, token government positions. (pp. 13–14)

Most policies aimed at desegregation or a redistribution of resources directly challenge white hegemony over the schools. Decentralization gives the illusion of change while threatening neither the racial make-up of the schools nor the financial arrangements of the wider society.

Orfield and Ashkinaze (1991) analyze the progress of African Americans in Atlanta and show that they have not made gains in employment, income, or education over the last two decades. These researchers document how the black leaders in Atlanta traded the desire for integration for more authority in the system; they "agreed to accept segregation in return for power within a deteriorating and increasingly isolated [educational] system" (p. 112). The result was that neither equal opportunity nor equal outcomes were a reality. They conclude, "The thesis that black politicians, conservative businessmen, and Atlanta's isolated low-income children had the same common long-term interests was wrong" (p. 148).

We read decentralization as a similar trade-off of resources for power. Decentralization is cast as the solution to the problem of unresponsive public school systems: If government is already the problem, then spending more money on bureaucracy cannot be the solution. This coincides with the conservative emphasis on no new taxes. Many decentralization advocates have suggested that school problems can be solved by changes in how schools are run, making school decentralization reforms revenue-neutral. National educational reform efforts (e.g., National Commission on Excellence in Education 1983) furthered this position with an emphasis on excellence rather than equity. Excellence supposedly required changes in practices, not in resources.

The final ideological result is an urban policy that meets many of the conditions for conservative government support. The irony is that racial cleavage between blacks and whites is inadvertently strengthened by liberal decentralization advocates. State legislators from suburban and rural districts can vote for racial separatism without concern for equity in resources. Equality and redistribution are seemingly transcended by changes in school organization and parent participation. What should be a natural liberal coalition of teachers and parents around a definition of the education problem as socioeconomic has instead been erased by the decentralization motif. The interests of parents and teachers are now disparate. The business elite can affiliate with those who represent black poor.

The strength and efficacy of this new conservative coalition depends in large measure on the power of different interests in both city and state politics, and there are important variations on the decentralization theme. But there can be little doubt that the traditional ways of thinking about how interest groups affect the government are inadequate to the decentralization phenomenon. As parents and community representatives take their place as part of the governance structure, interest groups are absorbed into the very government they are trying to influence.

Could decentralization have done more? From our vantage point, we think not. There is little doubt that some schools have been improved by decentralization efforts, but that is not enough. In terms of our two models, the empowerment model fails to specify the correct causes of school failure and the connections between those factors and policy innovation. Even if the model is implemented well, a tall order in and of itself, the exogenous factors that lead to the failure of the minority poor in school would be overpowering forces in the lives of children and would seem to require more than a change in school governance can deliver.

As we concluded our study in 1993, three of the five school systems we analyzed were without a superintendent. New York City, which had such high hopes for Chancellor Joseph Fernandez, did not renew his contract. Chicago, which worked to topple Manford Byrd, Jr., asked the replacement superintendent Ted Kimbrough to resign. And Los Angeles, which at the beginning of our study had just hired Dade County's superintendent Leonard Britton (and which had replaced him in 1990), was also searching for new leadership. It is not hard to understand why so many large urban school systems are searching for new leadership—it happens exactly when resources for these systems are not forthcoming. Chicago, for one, is facing a deficit of some $300 million. These systems search for new leadership but provide no additional funds. New forms of participation and the shifts in formal authority are mere "tinkerings." They mean little when neither leadership nor revenue is there to meet the challenges of poverty and racism. As the children of the United States lose their white complexion, it is time to move beyond decentralization. To wait much longer is to lose another generation.

Appendix

DATA COLLECTION IN THE FIVE CITIES

To explore the context of school reform in each of our study sites we utilized semistructured interviews consisting of two parts: a set of questions geared specifically toward the particular "type" of respondent (e.g., board member, reform organization) and a set of questions general to all respondents. The questions for our study were modeled and adapted from Crain's (1969) study *The Politics of School Desegregation* and focused on the educational reform process, current reform issues, and perceptions of leadership.

To generate our sample, we began with an initial list of educational leaders, political elites, and community representatives (these names were taken from articles or recommended by personal contacts); we added to each list based upon the recommendations of our respondents. From September 1988 through June 1989, visits were made to each study site to gather materials and to conduct interviews. Ninety-five percent of the interviews were performed in person, lasting from one half-hour to three hours.

In all, 27 interviews were done in Chicago, 24 in Detroit, 24 in Los Angeles, 20 in Dade County/Miami, and 22 in New York City. The racial breakdown of the sample was: 58 percent white, 28 percent black, and 14 percent Hispanic, Asian, or other.

Six "types" of respondents were interviewed: general superintendents, school board members, teachers union members, state political
leaders, city political leaders, and reform group members. Five interviews were done with general superintendents or representatives from
that office; every city's general superintendent was represented except
Chicago's. The total number of board members interviewed was 33: 5
in Chicago, 9 in Detroit, 6 in Los Angeles, 7 in Dade County, and 6 in
New York. We interviewed six teachers union members, two from
Dade County and one from every other city. Twenty-two state political leaders were interviewed, 10 from Chicago, 4 from Detroit, 4 from
Los Angeles, 3 from Dade County, and 1 from New York; state political leaders were mostly state representatives or state senators,
although legislative staff and state department of education superintendents or staff were also included in this group.

We also interviewed 10 city political leaders in the five cities: 3
from Dade County, 2 from Detroit, 2 from Los Angeles, 1 from Dade
County, and 2 from New York. Four of these respondents were on the
city council and six were currently on or had served on the mayor's
staff. Finally, 41 interviews with community reform groups were
completed, with 8 interviews from Chicago, 6 from Detroit, 10 from
Los Angeles, 6 from Dade County, and 11 from New York.

DATA COLLECTION IN CHICAGO

For the study of Chicago, a mix of quantitative and qualitative data
was gathered. First, semistructured and open-ended interviews were
done with members of the educational and civic elite. Readers might
be confused by the number of educational elite interviews done in
Chicago. The 27 Chicago interviews described above were done after
an initial set of 43 open-ended interviews done during the summer of
1988. The analysis in chapter 5 is based on these 43 interviews. Many
of the same people or representatives of the same organizations were
interviewed in both rounds (11 respondents were interviewed both
times). Table A.1 breaks down the sample of 43 by race and position.

The other data sources in Chicago were (1) the parent telephone
survey and (2) in-person parent interviews. These also generated a
mix of both quantitative and qualitative data.

Table A.1
Breakdown of 43 Chicago Open-Ended Interviews

	White	*Black*	*Hispanic*	*Total*
School board (Includes superintendent, board members, staff, consultants)	6	4	2	12
Reform group (Includes parents, businesspersons, and summit participants)	8	11	2	21
Politicians (Includes state and city legislators and staff)	6	2	0	8
Teachers union	1	1	0	2
Total	21	18	4	43

The Telephone Survey

To establish a general context of parent involvement, a random sample of 378 Chicago parents was chosen for a structured telephone survey, carried out by the Northwestern University telephone survey lab. Parents were identified through a random-digit dialing technique where all Chicago telephone number prefixes were entered into a computer and suffixes were then randomly generated. In this way, all households with a telephone had an equal probability of being selected, even those with unlisted telephone numbers. About 5 to 10 percent of Chicago households do not have phones. For the sample size we generated, the standard error is ±5 percent. In all, 378 interviews were completed, 26 of them in Spanish. In each household, we selected for the parent who had the most knowledge of the child's education; both public school and private school parents were included. The parent selected was then questioned about his or her involvement with respect to one particular child in the household. That child was chosen randomly based on the month of birth. This allowed for a random sample of parents involved in both elementary school and high

school, and forced the parent to think in specific terms about involvement with one particular child rather than all children in the household. Each survey took about twenty to thirty minutes to administer.

Of the 378 parents we interviewed in our phone survey, 253 were
parents of children in public schools, and 125 were parents with children in the private schools. Sixty-six percent (251) were parents with
a child in elementary school, the other 34 percent (127) were parents
with a child in high school. Most of the sample (80 percent) were
female. Over half (57 percent) of the sample had an income greater
than $20,000, and 49 percent reported an education of some college
or more.

Of the 253 public school parents, 48 percent (122) were black, 27
percent (68) were white, 21 percent (53) were Hispanic, and 4 percent
(10) were other. In comparison, this is the racial breakdown of the
Chicago public schools: blacks make up 60 percent of total public
school enrollment, whites make up 12 percent, Hispanics make up 25
percent, and Asians or other make up 3 percent.

The In-Person Interview

Fifty in-person interviews were conducted with individuals who had
been elected as parent representatives for their local school councils.
These interviews consisted of both the structured questions used in
the phone survey and a set of open-ended questions specifically about
the LSC experience.

To generate the sample for these interviews, a list of the 3,234
parents originally elected to the LSCs was obtained from the Chicago
Board of Education. Each parent on the list was assigned a number,
and a table of random numbers was used to select 108 parents, of
whom 50 were interviewed. Parents controlled where the interviews
were done; most interviews took place at the respondent's home, and
a few took place in restaurants or at other public places. Interviews
lasted from forty-five minutes to four hours, and the open-ended por-
tions were audiotaped and transcribed.

For the 50 in-person interviews, 48 percent (24) were black, 32
percent (16) were white, 18 percent (9) were Hispanic, and 2 percent
(1) was Asian. Eighty-eight percent of the parents were from elementary schools, and 70 percent were female. The majority of the sample

(66 percent) had a total household income of more than $20,000. The average age was forty-one years old, and 68 percent (34) of the respondents were married. Twenty-two percent of the in-person interviews were with parents with a college degree or postgraduate work; 50 percent of the sample had some college. And 74 percent of these parents had attended a Chicago public school for part or all of their kindergarten through high school education.

Open-ended questions for the in-person interview were developed after preliminary interviews with parents and participation in a variety of parent training workshops. Questions for the structured survey covered four areas: school satisfaction, perception of problems, educational attitudes, and parent involvement. These were adapted from other studies on parent involvement and are described below.

1. *Questions on school satisfaction* (adapted from Marjoribanks 1978; Rosenbaum and Popkin 1990). Parents in both the telephone survey and the LSC in-person interviews were asked how satisfied they were with various aspects of their child's schooling. Twelve different areas were discussed: the school overall, the quality of teaching, the way teachers treated their child, the help teachers gave their child, the size of classes, the amount the child was expected to learn, afterschool activities, the amount of information the school provided about how the child was doing, the way the school and grounds looked, school maintenance and cleanliness, the amount of discipline, and the amount of time spent on reading and math. Parents were asked whether they were very satisfied, somewhat satisfied, somewhat dissatisfied or very dissatisfied. Public school parents in the telephone interview and the LSC parents were also asked how satisfied they were with how school reform was working in their school.

2. *Questions on school problems.* Parents in both the LSC in-person interviews and the telephone survey were read a list of issues and asked if they considered the issue a big problem, some problem, or almost no problem at their child's school. The issues asked about were resources, parent involvement, dropout rate, student achievement, disinterested teachers, education of non-English-speaking students, education of low-income students, drugs, gang violence, and children's safety in and out of the school. The issues were drawn from the semistructured interviews with Chicago policy makers, communi-

ty organizers, parents, and board members, who were asked to identify three major educational issues in Chicago.

3. *Educational attitudes* (adapted from Epstein and Becker 1987). Both LSC parents and telephone survey parents were asked whether they strongly agreed, somewhat agreed, somewhat disagreed, or strongly disagreed with a series of fourteen statements. The statements covered the parent's attitudes toward their child's education and how well a child learns. Other statements measured a parent's perceptions of the utility of parent involvement. Parents were also asked to assess the school climate. The questions were used to paint a broader picture of the parents in Chicago and their attitudes toward education.

4. *Measures of parent involvement* (adapted from Epstein and Becker 1987; Oyemade and Washington 1985; School District Survey #300; *Chicago Crime Prevention Evaluation Survey, Wave II* 1979). We asked parents a variety of questions covering their involvement in school activities. These questions were utilized only for the telephone survey. Parents were specifically asked about eight different school activities. First, we inquired whether they had heard of an activity taking place at their school, and if they had heard of the activity, we asked if they were able to take part in the activity. The eight activities were observing in the classroom, helping the teacher in the class or on a trip, helping with a birthday or other class party, providing materials for the classroom, helping in the library or cafeteria or playground or office, helping with fund-raising, serving on a school committee, and serving as a school representative to some other organization. Other yes/no questions covered whether parents had attended a meeting at the school and whether the parent had taken part in any other kinds of activities at the school.

References

Anderson, A. B., & Pickering, G. W. (1986). *Confronting the color line: The broken promise of the civil rights movement in Chicago.* Athens: University of Georgia.

Anderson, C. W. (1979). Political design and the representation of interests. In P. C. Schmitter & G. Lehmbruch (Eds.), *Trends toward corporatist intermediation* (pp. 271–97). London: Sage.

Banfield, E. C., & Wilson, J. Q. (1963). *City politics.* Cambridge: Harvard University Press.

Bastian, A., Fruchter, N., Gittell, M., Greer, C., & Haskins, K. (1986). *Choosing equality: The case for democratic schooling.* Philadelphia: Temple University.

Becker, H. J., & Epstein, J. L. (1982). Parent involvement: A study of teacher practices. *The Elementary School Journal, 83,* 85–102.

Becker, H. S. (1963). *Outsiders: Studies in the sociology of deviance.* London: Free Press.

Bell, D. (1992). *Faces at the bottom of the well: The permanence of racism.* New York: Basic Books.

Bendiner, R. (1969). *The politics of schools, a crisis in self government.* New York: Harper & Row.

Berger, J. (1992, 26 June). Reading and math scores drop across New York. *New York Times,* pp. B1, B4.

Berube, M. R. (1969). The unschooling of New York's children. In M. R. Berube & M. Gittell (Eds.), *Confrontation at Ocean Hill–Brownsville: The New York school strikes of 1968* (pp. 136–38). New York: Praeger.

Berube, M. R., & Gittell, M. (Eds). (1969). *Confrontation at Ocean Hill–Brownsville: The New York school strikes of 1968.* New York: Praeger.

Bowles, S., & Gintis, H. (1976). *Schooling in capitalist America: Educational reform and the contradictions of modern life.* New York: Basic Books.

Boyd, W. L., & O'Shea, D. W. (1975). Theoretical perspectives on school district decentralization. *Education and Urban Society, 7* (4), 357–76.

Bresnick, D. (1974). Cyclical renewal in a large city school district—decentralization and the policy process. *Educational Administration Quarterly, 10,* 19–34.

Brodt, B. (1988, 20 November). School reform's Achilles heel: The parents. *Chicago Tribune,* pp. 1, 4.

Brown, D. J. (1990). *Decentralization and school based management.* New York: Falmer.

Browning, R. P., Marshall, D. G., & Tabb, D. H. (1984). *Protest is not enough: The struggle of blacks and Hispanics for equality in urban politics.* Berkeley: University of California Press.

Burnham, J. (1943). *The Machiavellians.* New York: John Day.

Burnham, J. (1985). *Suicide of the West: An essay on the meaning and destiny of liberalism.* Chicago: Gateway Editions.

Caldwell, B. J., & Spinks, J. M. (1988). *The self-managing school.* New York: Falmer.

Carmichael, S., & Hamilton, C. V. (1967). *Black power: The politics of liberation in America.* New York: Random House.

Caughey, J., & Caughey, L. (1969). Decentralization of the Los Angeles schools: Front for segregation. *Integrated education: A Report on Race and Schools, 7* (5), 48–51.

Cawson, A. (1986). *Corporatism and political theory.* Oxford: Basil Blackwell.

Cervone, B. T., & O'Leary, K. (1982). A conceptual framework for parent involvement. *Educational Leadership, 40* (2), 48–49.

Chicago crime prevention evaluation survey, wave II. (1979). Evanston: Northwestern University Survey Research Lab.

Chicago Panel on Public School Policy and Finance. (1988). *Chicago plans for reform for the Chicago public schools.* Chicago: Author.

Chicago Panel on Public School Policy and Finance. (1990). *Chicago public schools databook* (school year 1988–89). Chicago: Author.

Chicago Panel on Public School Policy and Finance. (1991). *Panel update, VII* (5), 10–11.

Chicago School Reform, Illinois Public Act 85-1418. (1988).

Chicago School Reform Training Task Force. (1989). *Kids first: Leadership guide for school reform.* Chicago: Author.

Chicago Teachers Union. (1988, July). *Update.* Chicago: Author.

Cistone, P. J., Fernandez, J. A., & Tornillo, P. L. (1989). School-based management/shared decision making in Dade County (Miami). *Education and Urban Society, 21,* 393–402.

Clark, K. B. (1965). *Dark ghetto: Dilemmas of social power.* New York: Harper & Row.

Clark, K. B. (1970). Introduction. In M. Fantini, M. Gittell, & R. Magat, *Community control and the urban school* (pp. ix–xi). New York: Praeger.

Clarke, S. E. (1986). Urban America incorporated: Corporatist convergence of power in American cities? In E. M. Bergman (Ed.), *Local economics in transition.* Durham, N.C.: Duke University Press.

Cohen, A. M. (1966). The process of desegregation: A case study. *Journal of Negro Education, 35,* 445–51.

Cohen, D. (1978). Reforming school politics. *Harvard Educational Review, 48,* 429–47.

Cohen, W. (1973). Policy and politics in education. *School Review, 82* (1), 127–29.

Coleman, J. S. (1990). *Parent involvement in education.* Paper presented at the United States Department of Education. University of Chicago, Sociology Department.

Comer, J. P. (1980). *School power: Implications for an intervention project.* New York: Free Press.

Comer, J. P. (1986). Parent participation in the schools. *Phi Delta Kappan, 67* (6), 442–46.

Crain, R. (1969). *The politics of school desegregation.* Garden City, N.Y.: Anchor Books.

Cunningham, L. L., et al. (1978). *Improving education in Florida: A reassessment.* Prepared for the Select Joint Committee on Public Schools of the Florida Legislature. Tallahassee: Florida State Legislature.

Dauer, M. J. (Ed.). (1984). *Florida's politics and government.* Gainesville: University of Florida Press.

Detroit Public Schools. (1989). *Dropout, graduation, and retention for new ninth graders 1982, 1983, 1984.* Detroit: Office of Data Management, Department of Student Information Services.

Dimond, P. R. (1985). *Beyond busing: Inside the challenge to urban segregation.* Ann Arbor: University of Michigan Press.

Drake, S. C., & Cayton, H. R. (1945). *Black metropolis: A study of Negro life in a Northern city.* New York: Harcourt, Brace.

Easton, D. (1965). *A systems analysis of political life.* New York: John Wiley.

Easton, J. Q., Storey, S. L., Johnson, C., Qualls, J., & Ford, D. (1990). *Local school council meetings during the first year of Chicago school reform.* Chicago: Chicago Panel on Public School Finance.

Eckstein, H. (1984). Civic inclusion and its discontents. *Daedalus, 113* (4), 107–45.

Elmore, R. F. (1979–80). Backward mapping: Implementation research and policy decisions. *Political Science Quarterly, 94* (4), 601–16.

Elmore, R. F. (1991). Foreward. In G. A. Hess, *School Restructuring, Chicago Style* (pp. vii–ix). Newbury Park, Calif.: Corwin.

Epstein, J. L. (1985). Home and school connections in schools for the future: Implications of research on parent involvement. *Peabody Journal of Education, 62* (2), 18–41.

Epstein, J. L. (1993). A response [to *[Ap]parent involvement*]. *Teachers College Record, 94* (4), 710–17.

Epstein J. L., & Becker, H. J. (1987). *Hopkins surveys of schools and family connections: Questionnaires for teachers, parents, and students.* Baltimore: Johns Hopkins University, Center for Research on Elementary and Middle Schools.

Fantini, M., Gittell, M., & Magat, R. (1970). *Community control and the urban school.* New York: Praeger.

Fine, M. (1993). [Ap]parent involvement: Reflections on parents, power, and urban public schools. *Teachers College Record, 94* (4), 682–710.

Fine, M., & Cook, D. (1992). *Evaluation reports: "With and for parents."* Washington, D.C.: William T. Grant Foundation.

Florida Department of Education. (1988). *Dropouts by school, grades 9–12, school year 86–87.* Tallahassee: Author.

Fredrickson, G. M. (1971). *The black image in the white mind.* Middletown, Conn.: Wesleyan University.

Gittell, M. (1972). Decentralization and citizen participation in education. *Public Administration Review, 32,* 670–86.

Gittell, M., & Berube, M. R. (1971). *Demonstration for social change: An experiment in local control.* New York: Queens College of the City of University of New York, Institute for Community Studies.

Gittell, M., & Hevesi, A. G. (Eds.). (1969). *The politics of urban education.* New York: Praeger.

Glass, T. E., & Sanders, W. D. (1978). *Community control in education.* Midland, Mo.: Pendell.

Goffman, E. (1961). *Asylums: Essays on the social situation of mental patients and other inmates.* Garden City, N.Y.: Anchor Books.

Goodlad, J. I. (1984). *A place called school: Prospects for the future.* New York: McGraw-Hill.

Gordon, I. J. (1977). Parent education and parent involvement: Retrospect and prospect. *Childhood Education, 54* (1), 71–79.

Grant, W. R. (1971). Community control vs. integration: The case of Detroit. *Public Interest, 24,* 62–79.

Green, R. L. (1973). Community control and desegregation. *School review, 81* (3), 347–56.

Green, R. L. (1974). Northern school desegregation: Educational, legal, and political issues. In C. W. Gordon (Ed.), *Uses of the sociology of education* (pp. 213–72). Chicago: University of Chicago Press.

Greenstone, J. D., & Peterson, P. E. (1968). Reformers, machines, and the War on Poverty. In J. Q. Wilson (Ed.), *City politics and public policy* (pp. 267–92). New York: John Wiley.

Greenstone, J. D., & Peterson, P. E. (1973). *Race and authority in urban politics: Community participation and the War on Poverty.* New York: Sage.

Gruber, J., & Trickett, E. J. (1987). Can we empower others? The paradox of empowerment in the governing of an alternative public school. *American Journal of Community Psychology, 15* (3), 353–71.

Hamilton, C. V. (1969). Race and education: A search for legitimacy. In *Equal educational opportunity* (pp. 187–202). Cambridge: Harvard University Press.

Harlem Youth Opportunities Unlimited. (1964). *Youth in the ghetto: A study of the consequences of powerlessness and a blueprint for change.* New York: Author.

Havighurst, R. J. (1964). *The public schools of Chicago—a survey for the board of education of the city of Chicago.* Chicago: Chicago Board of Education.

Hess, G. A. (1991). *School restructuring, Chicago style.* Newbury Park, Calif.: Corwin.

Hochschild, J. L. (1984). *The new American dilemma: Liberal democracy and school desegregation.* New Haven: Yale University Press.

HOPE. (1988). Position statement for Frank Hayden, David Olmstead, and Larry Patrick, Detroit Board of Education. Mimeographed.

Katz, M. B. (1971). *Class, bureaucracy, and schools: The illusion of educational change in America.* New York: Praeger.

Katz, M. B. (1992). Chicago school reform as history. *Teachers College Record, 94,* 56–72.

Katznelson, I. (1981). *City trenches: Urban politics and the patterning of class in the United States.* New York: Pantheon Books.

Katznelson, I., & Weir, M. (1985). *Schooling for all: Class, race, and the decline of the democratic ideal.* New York: Basic Books.

Kimbrough, R., Alexander, K., & Wattenberger, J. (1984). Government and education. In M. J. Dauer (Ed.), *Florida's politics and government* (pp. 422–47). Gainesville: University of Florida Press.

LaNoue, G. R., & Smith, B. L. R. (1971). The political evolution of school decentralization. *American Behavioral Scientist, 15* (1), 73–93.

LaNoue, G. R., & Smith, B. L. R. (1973). *The politics of school decentralization.* Lexington, Mass.: Lexington Books.

Lederman, N. M., Franckl, J. S., & Baum, J. (1987). *Governing the New York City schools: Roles and relationships in the decentralized system.* New York: Board of Trustees of Public Education Association.

Leler, H. (1983). Parent education and involvement in relation to the schools and to parents of school-aged children. In R. Haskins & D. Adams (Eds.), *Parent education and public policy* (pp. 141–80). Norwood, N.J.: Ablex.

Lemann, N. (1991). *The promised land: The great black migration and how it changed America.* New York: Knopf.

Lenz, L. (1989, September). An authoritative guide to school reform. *Chicago Enterprise,* p. 19.

Levin, H. (Ed.). (1970). *Community control of schools.* New York: Clarion.

Levinsohn, F. H. (1989, 26 May). School revolt. *Reader,* pp. 1, 18, 20, 22, 24, 26–29.

Lewis, D. A., Grant, J. A., & Rosenbaum, D. P. (1988). *Social construction of reform: Crime prevention and community organizations.* New Brunswick: Transaction Books.

Lightfoot, S. L. (1978). *Worlds apart: Relationships between families and schools.* New York: Basic Books.

Lighthall, F. F. (1989). *Local realities, local adaptations: Problem, process, and person in a school's governance.* New York: Falmer.

Lind, E. A., & Tyler, T. R. (1988). *The social psychology of procedural justice.* New York: Plenum Press.

Lipset, S. M. (1963). *Political man: The social bases of politics.* Garden City, N.Y.: Doubleday.

Los Angeles Unified School District. (1988). *CTBS test scores: Norm-referenced test results.* Los Angeles: Author.

Luddy, K. (1988, October). Proposition 98: School funding for instructional improvement and accountability. *California Journal, Propositions,* pp. 10–11.

Lyke, R. F. (1970). Representation and urban school boards. In H. M. Levin (Ed.), *Community control of schools.* Washington, D.C.: Brookings Institution.

Malen, B., & Ogawa, R. (1988). Professional-patron influence on site-based governance councils: A confounding case study. *Educational Evaluation and Policy Analysis, 10* (4), 251–70.

Manhattan Borough President's Task Force on Education and Decentralization. (1987). *Improving the odds: Making decentralization work for children, for schools, for communities.* New York: Author.

Marjoribanks, K. (1978). Ethnicity, family environment, school attitudes and academic achievement. *Australian Journal of Education, 22* (3), 249–61.

Marris, P., & Rein, M. (1967). *Dilemmas of social reform.* Chicago: University of Chicago Press.

Massell, D., & Kirst, M. W. (1985). State policymaking for educational excellence: School reform in California. In V. D. Mueller & M. McKeown (Eds.), *The fiscal, legal, and political aspects of state reform of elementary and secondary education* (pp. 121–44). Cambridge, Mass.: Ballinger.

Mayor's Advisory Panel on Decentralization of the New York City Public Schools. (1969). Reconnection for learning (the Bundy Report). In M. Gittell & A. G. Hevesi (Eds.), *The politics of urban education* (pp. 261–76). New York: Praeger.

McBay, S. M. (1992). The condition of African American education: Changes and challenges. In B. J. Tidwell (Ed.), *The state of black America* (pp. 141–56). New York: National Urban League.

McClory, R. (1987, February). Manford Byrd's report card. *Chicago Magazine,* 125–30.

McKersie, W. S. (1993). Philanthropy's paradox: Chicago school reform. *Educational Evaluation and Policy Analysis, 15* (2), 109–28.

McLaughlin, M. W., & Shields, P. M. (1987). Involving low-income parents in the schools: A role for policy? *Phi Delta Kappan, 69,* 156–60.

Meyer, J. W. (1977). The effects of education as an institution. *American Journal of Sociology, 83* (1), 55–77.

Morone, J. A. (1990). *The democratic wish: Popular participation and the limits of American government.* New York: Basic Books.

Myrdal, G. (1944). *An American dilemma: The Negro problem and modern democracy.* New York: Harper.

National Commission on Excellence in Education. (1983). *A nation at risk.* Washington, D.C.: U.S. Government Printing Office.

Nazario, S. L. (1989, 31 March). Failing in 81 languages. *Wall Street Journal,* pp. R21–R22.

New York City Board of Education. (1987). *The 1985–86 dropout report.* New York: Author.

Nye, B. A. (1989). Effective parent education and involvement models and programs: Contemporary strategies for school implementation. In M. J. Fine (Ed.), *The second handbook on parent education: Contemporary perspectives* (pp. 325–45). New York: Academic Press.

O'Connell, M. (1991). *School reform Chicago style: How citizens organized to change public policy.* Chicago: Center for Neighborhood Technology.

Odden, A., & Marsh, D. (1988). How comprehensive reform legislation can improve secondary schools. *Phi Delta Kappan, 69,* 593–98.

Ogbu, J. U. (1978). *Minority education and caste: The American system in cross-cultural perspective.* New York: Academic Press.

Ogbu, J. U. (1992). Understanding cultural diversity and learning. *Educational Researcher, 21* (8), 5–14, 24.

Orfield, G. (1978). *Must we bus? Segregated schools and national policy.* Washington, D.C.: Brookings Institution.

Orfield, G. (1984). Lessons of the Los Angeles desegregation case. *Education and Urban Society, 16* (3), 338–53.

Orfield, G., & Ashkinaze, C. (1991). *The closing door: Conservative policy and black opportunity.* Chicago: University of Chicago Press.

Ornstein, A. C. (1973). Administrative/community organization of metropolitan schools. *Phi Delta Kappan, 54,* 668–74.

Ornstein, A. C. (1983). Administrative decentralization and community policy: Review and outlook. *Urban Review, 15* (1), 3–10.

O'Shea, D. W. (1975). School district decentralization: The case of Los Angeles. *Education and Urban Society, 7* (4), 377–92.

Oyemade, U. J., & Washington, V. (1985). Parent survey. Unpublished manuscript. Washington, D.C.: Howard University.

Pellicano, R. R. (1985). The decentralization of New York City's public schools. [Review of *110 Livingston Street revisited: Decentralization in action* and *Across the river: Politics and education in the city*]. *Urban Education, 19* (4), 447–51.

Perlez, J. (1988, 12 March). Assembly chief seeks to cut power of New York school board. *New York Times*, p. 9.

Peterson, P. E. (1976). *School politics, Chicago style.* Chicago: University of Chicago Press.

Peterson, P. E. (1985). *The politics of school reform: 1870–1940.* Chicago: University of Chicago Press.

Piven, F. F., & Cloward, R. A. (1971). *Regulating the poor: The functions of public welfare.* New York: Pantheon Books.

Purkey, S., & Smith, M. (1983). Effective schools: A review. *Elementary School Journal, 83,* 428–52.

Ravitch, D. (1974). *The great school wars: A history of the New York City public schools.* New York: Basic Books.

Ravitch, D., & Grant, W. R. (1975). School decentralization in New York City 1975 [and] Detroit's experience with school decentralization. Washington, D.C.: Center for Governmental Studies. (ERIC Document Reproduction Service No. ED 113 428)

Rogers, D. (1968). *110 Livingston Street.* New York: Random House.

Rogers, D. (1982). School decentralization: It works. *Social Policy, 12,* 13–23.

Rogers, D., & Chung, N. H. (1983). *110 Livingston Street revisited: Decentralization in action.* New York: New York University Press.

Rosenbaum, J. E., & Popkin, S. J. (1990). *Economic and social impacts of housing integration* (working paper). Evanston, Ill.: Center for Urban Affairs and Policy Research, Northwestern University.

Rungeling, B., & Glover, R. W. (1991). Educational restructuring—the process for change? *Urban Education, 25* (4), 415–27.

Salisbury, R. (1980). *Citizen participation in the schools.* Lexington, Mass.: Lexington Books.

Schmalz, J. (1989, 21 March). Miami students: Future's hope, today's crisis. *New York Times,* p. A1.

Schmitter, P. C. (1979). Still the century of corporatism? In P. C. Schmitter & G. Lehmbruch (Eds.), *Trends toward corporatist intermediation* (pp. 7–52). London: Sage.

School District Survey #300. (n.d.) Evanston, Ill.: Northwestern University Survey Research Lab.

Scribner, J. D., & O'Shea, D. (1974). Political developments in urban school districts. In C. W. Gordon (Ed.), *Uses of the sociology of education* (pp. 380–407). Chicago: University of Chicago Press.

Selznick, P. (1949). *TVA and the grass roots.* Berkeley: University of California Press.

Shils, E. A. (1982). *The constitution of society.* Chicago: University of Chicago Press.

Sitkoff, H. (1978). *A new deal for blacks.* New York: Oxford University Press.

Slaughter, D. T., & Kuehne, V. S. (1988). Improving black education: Perspectives on parental involvement. *Urban League Review, 11* (1–2), 59–75.

Snider, W. (1989, August 2). Proposition 98 nets California schools a 12.5 percent increase in state funds. *Education Week,* p. 15.

Snider, W. (1990, 21 November). Parents as partners: Adding their voices to decisions on how schools are run. *Education Week,* pp. 11–20.

Stevenson, D. L., & Baker, D. P. (1987). The family-school relation and the child's school performance. *Child Development, 58,* 1348–57.

Taylor, D. G. (1986). *Public opinion and collective action: The Boston school desegregation conflict.* Chicago: University of Chicago Press.

Tyack, D. B. (1974). *The one best system: A history of American urban education.* Cambridge: Harvard University Press.

U.S. Department of Labor. (1989). Washington, D.C.: Labor Management Services Administration, Division of Public Employee Labor Relations.

Valentine, J., & Stark, E. (1979). The social context of parent involvement in Head Start. In E. Zigler & J. Valentine (Eds.), *Project Head Start: A legacy of the War on Poverty* (pp. 291–314). New York: Free Press.

Wasley, P. (1993). A response [to *[Ap]parent involvement]*. *Teachers College Record, 94* (4), 720–27.

Weber, M. (1946). *From Max Weber: Essays in sociology.* New York: Oxford University Press.

White, J. B. (1988, 11 November). Failures of Detroit schools spur revolt as three longtime officials are ousted. *Wall Street Journal,* p. A16.

Wilner, R. (1987). Agenda for the next chancellor of the New York City public schools. *Citizens Budget Commission Quarterly, 7* (4), 16–24.

Wohlstetter, P., & McCurdy, K. (1991). The link between school decentralization and school politics. *Urban Education, 25* (4), 391–414.

Woo, E. (1988, 21 June). Schools: Judge orders desegregation lawsuit settled. *Los Angeles Times,* pp. I1, I16.

Zigler, E., & Valentine, J. (Eds.). (1979). *Project Head Start: A legacy of the War on Poverty.* New York: Free Press.

Author Index

193

Subject Index